Crypto

Learning How to Invest and Estimate with Cryptocurrencies

By Johnnie Alberts

Copyright @2019

If you like my book, please leave a review. I would appreciate it a lot. Thanks!

Table of Contents

Model Management

Release and embed countless predictive models straight into service procedures.

Scale and preserve peak efficiency for every single model and schedule updates as needed.

Manage the whole predictive modeling lifecycle from information prep to model structure, assessment, implementation, and tracking.

Predictive Modeling

Build predictive models in days with automation and setup functions no coding needed.

Gain simple access to a variety of artificial intelligence algorithms.

Benefit from native predictive modeling with Big Data.

Predictive Data Management

Speed up information preparation and join historic information sets like demographics, deals, and service calls.

Produce and manage huge analytical datasets with as much as 50,000 columns.

Increase your capability to obtain more precise and foreseeable actual results.

Predictive Network and Link Analysis

Represent information in charts to show item or entity associations.

Extract and check out links between your clients and social influencers.

Create item suggestions based upon social media analysis.

Usage geo-referenced information to build models and picture the most-visited geographical places.

Scoring

Rating information much faster and use predictive models in databases, as quickly as events take place.

Create code for a range of target databases.

Embed precise predictive actual results into organisation procedures.

Predictive Analytics: Surpass Charts

Data Science within your reaches

Without writing any code, users can point-and-click to get immediate connected views, one-click forecasts, and proactive information profiles. All users have access to the exact same sophisticated computations that your specialists have, so everybody can be more effective and ultimately more knowledgeable and smarter. In a way, Spotfire lets you break information science out of its box and proclaim.

Embed R Code In Analyses

Since Area fire has a natively ingrained R engine, it can run the world's most well-known open source analytical language straight inside any analysis. It offers point-and-click authoring for users of all levels, and offers advanced users the capability to run customized R models in the analysis.

Let Your Information Researchers Empower the Company

Area fire consists of the right tools for making it much easier for specialists to resolve an issue then release their resolution as analytical apps that can be recycled by everybody. Rather than losing time by keeping the value of your information science financial investments to a little corner of your business, you can optimize that value and make both specialists and no specialists more effective. And you can empower the exact same people who comprehend the issue to work the resolution.

Utilize Your Existing Platforms

Link to existing information functions written in R, SAS, and MATLAB. Helped by the special and effective Area fire Data Providers Engine, users at big can then gain from your saved properties, and you won't have a stranded financial investment.

Anticipate the future

Your huge information is only as great as your capability to use it to anticipate, produce a strategy, and act upon it. What item should you advise for purchase at this moment? Is scams being tried? Which device needs upkeep to stay away from a blockage? What enhancements can you make to extend item life? Who's at risk of entering into heart attack? Area fire gives you quick answers.

One-click Stats

Contextual estimations make effective techniques simple to use: detailed statistics, resemblance, clustering, connections, fitting, and projection.

You can save real analyses, not just control panels, for usage by all. In Spotfire, creating apps is an integrated function. For other items, it's out of reach.

Some Advantages and Dangers of Bitcoin

Among the advantages of Bitcoin is its low inflation danger. Standard currencies experience inflation and they tend to lose their buying power each year, as federal governments continue to use quantative relieving to promote the economy.

Bitcoin does not struggle with low inflation, as Bitcoin mining is restricted to just 21 million systems. That means the release of brand-new Bitcoins is decreasing and the total will be mined out within the next number of years. Professionals have forecasted that the last Bitcoin will be mined by 2050.

Bitcoin has a low threat of collapse in contrast to standard currencies that depend on federal governments. When currencies collapse, it causes run-away inflation or the wipeout of one's cost savings in an immediate.

Bitcoin currency exchange rate is not controlled by any federal government and is a digital currency readily available around the world.

Bitcoin is simple to carry. A billion dollars in the Bitcoin can be saved on a memory stick and put in one's pocket. It is that simple to transfer Bitcoins compared to fiat money.

One downside of Bitcoin is its untraceable nature, as Federal governments and other organisations cannot trace the source of your funds and as such can bring in some unethical people.

How to Generate Income with Bitcoin

Unlike other currencies, there are 3 methods to earn money with Bitcoin, saving , trading and mining. Bitcoin can be traded on free markets, which means you can purchase Bitcoin low and sell them high.

Volatility of Bitcoin

The value of Bitcoin dropped in current weeks just because of the abrupt interruption of trading in Mt. Gox, which is the biggest Bitcoin exchange worldwide. According to unproven sources, trading was stopped as a result of malleability-related theft that was said to be worth more than 744,000. The event has impacted the self-confidence of the financiers to the virtual currency.

According to Bitcoin chart, the Bitcoin currency exchange rate went up to more than $1,100 last December. That was when more people realised about the digital currency, then the occurrence with Mt. Gox took place and it dropped to around $530.

In 2014, we expect rapid development in the appeal of bitcoin around the globe with merchants and customers, Stephen Set, Bit Pay's co-founder and CTO, and prepare for seeing the largest development in China, India, Russia and South America.

India has already been pointed out as the next very likely well-known market that Bitcoin could move into. Africa could also benefit extremely from using BTC as a currency-of-exchange to navigate not having an operating reserve bank system or any other nation that relies greatly on mobile payments. Bitcoin's growth in 2014 will be led by Bitcoin ATMs, mobile apps and tools.

Chapter 3: World Experiences Bitcoin

More people have accepted using Bitcoin and fans hope that one day, the digital currency will be used by customers for their online shopping and other electronic offers. Significant businesses have already accepted payments using the virtual currency. Some of the big companies consist of Fiverr, TigerDirect and Zynga, to name a few.

The Future of Bitcoin

Bitcoin works, but critics have said that the digital currency is not all set to be used by the mainstream just because of its volatility. They also indicate the hacking of the Bitcoin exchange in the past that has led to the loss of some countless dollars.

Advocates of digital currencies have said that there are more recent exchanges that are monitored by economists and investor. Specialists added that there is still hope for the virtual currency system and the anticipated development is big.

How to Purchase Bitcoin - Step One

The best way to find out about bitcoin, is to leap in and get several in your "pocket" to get a feel for how they work.

Regardless of the buzz about how challenging and unsafe it can be, getting bitcoins is a lot much easier and much safer than you may believe. In a ton of methods, it is most likely simpler than opening an account at a conventional bank. And, given what has been going on in the banking system, it is most likely much safer too.

There are several things to discover: getting and using a software application wallet, learning how to send out and get cash, learning how to purchase bitcoin from an individual or an exchange.

Preparation

Right before getting going, you will really need to get yourself a wallet. You can do this quickly adequate by signing up with among the exchanges which will host wallet for you. And, though I believe you are going to want to have several exchange wallets ultimately, you should begin with one by yourself computer system both to get a much better feel for bitcoin and since the exchanges are still speculative themselves. When we get to that phase of the conversation, I will be advising that you get in the practice of moving your cash and coins off the exchanges or diversifying right across exchanges to keep your cash safe.

Chapter 4: What is a Crypto Wallet?

It is a way to keep your bitcoins. Particularly, it is software application that has been developed to keep bitcoin. It can be operated on your desktop, laptop computer, mobile phone (other than, yet, Apple) and can also be made to save bitcoins on things like thumb drives. If you are concerned about being hacked, then that is a really good choice. Even the Winklevoss * twins, who have millions purchased bitcoin, put their financial investment on disk drives which they then took into a safe-deposit box.

* The Winklevoss twins are the ones who initially had the idea for a social networking site that ended up being Face book. They worked with Mark Zuckerberg who took their idea as his own and ended up being tremendously wealthy.

What do you really need to know about having a bitcoin wallet on your computer system?

Beneath you can download the initial bitcoin wallet, or customer, in Windows or Mac format. These are not just wallets, but are in simple fact part of the bitcoin network. They will get, shop, and send your bitcoins. You can produce several addresses with a click (an address is a number that appears like this: 1LyFcQatbg4BvT9gGTz6VdqqHKpPn5QBuk). You will see a field where you can copy and paste a number like this from an individual you want to send out cash to and off it will go straight into that person's wallet. You can even produce a QR code which will let somebody take an image with an app on their phone and send you some bitcoin. It is flawlessly safe to give these out - the address and QR code are both for my contributions page. Do not hesitate to contribute!

KEEP IN MIND: This kind of wallet acts both as a wallet for you and as part of the bitcoin system. The reason bitcoin works is that every deal is transmitted and made a record of as a number right across the whole system (meaning that every deal is validated and made permanent by the network itself). Any computer system with the right software application can be part of that system, examining and supporting the network. This wallet acts as your individual wallet and also as an help for that system. For that reason, know that it will use up 8-9 gigabytes of your computer system's memory. After you set up the wallet, it will take as much as a day for the wallet to sync with the network. This is typical, doesn't hurt your computer system, and makes the system as a whole more safe, so it's a very good idea.

Chapter 5: About Bitcoin Qt

The initial wallet

This is a full-featured wallet: develop several addresses to get bitcoins, send out bitcoins quickly, track deals, and back up your wallet.

Beyond the time it requires to sync, this is a really simple to use alternative.

Look For Bitcoin Qt wallet download to find their site.

Armory

Operates on top of Bitcoi Qt, so it has all of the exact same syncing requirements.

Armory enables you to back, secure, and the capability to save your bitcoins offline.

Look For Bitcoin Armory Wallet to find their site.

If you do not want to have that much memory used or do not want to wait on your wallet to sync, there are great wallets that do not make you sync the whole history of bitcocin:

Multibit

A light-weight wallet that synchronizes rapidly. This is great for brand-new users.

Look For Bitcoin Multibit Wallet to find their site.

Electum

In addition to fasting and light, this wallet permits you to recuperate lost information using a passcode.

Look For Bitcoin Electum Wallet to find their site.

After you get the wallet established, take several minutes clicking around. Things to search for:

There will be a page that shows you how many bitcoins are presently in your wallet. Remember that bitcoins can be separated into tinier pieces, so you might see a decimal with a ton of absolutely nos after it. (Intriguing note, 0.00000001 is one Satoshi, called after the pseudonymous developer of bitcoin).

There will be a region demonstrating what your current deals are.

There will be a part where you can develop an address and a QR code. You do not really need the QR code if you do not really want it, but if you run a firm and you want to accept bitcoin, then all you'll really need to do to accept payment is to show somebody the QR code, let them take an image of it, and they will have the ability to send you some cash. You will also have the ability to develop as lots of addresses as you like, so if you want to track where the cash is originating from, you could have an independently identified address from each one of your payees.

There will be a spot with a box for you to paste a code when you want to send out cash to somebody or to yourself on an exchange or different wallet.

There will be other alternatives and functions, but to begin with, these are the products that you should know about.

Chapter 6: Getting Your Very First Bitcoins

Now that you have a wallet, you will, obviously, want to check them out.

This is a site that provides percentages of bitcoin for the purpose of getting people used to using them. The initial variation of the was run by the lead designer of bitcoin, Gavin Anderson. That site has since closed and this site runs by sending a couple of ads a month. You consent to get those messages by asking for the bitcoins. Copy and paste your brand-new bitcoin address and go into a contact number to which you can get an SMS. They send an SMS to be sure that people are not constantly returning for more since it costs absolutely nothing to produce a bitcoin address. They will also send one or two times a month ad to support their operation. The amount they send it unimportant: 0.0015 BTC (or 1.5 mBTC). Nevertheless, they process practically instantly and you can check to see that your address and wallet are working. It is also rather some feeling to get that part of a bitcoin.

Congratulations! You have just gone into the bitcoin economy.

To get your feet a little wetter, you can go panning for gold. There are certain services and sites out there that will pay you in bitcoin to do things like go to certain sites, submit online studies, or watch sponsored videos. These are safe, and you can make several additional bitcoins that way, but it is crucial to bear in mind that these are organisations that make money when people click the links on their sites. They are basically settling back a part of what they make money to you. There is absolutely nothing prohibited, or perhaps unethical about this (you may like what you see and buy!), but they are often fancy and might not be entirely simple. All the ones that have tried (especially bitvisitor.com) have paid as promoted. It is fascinating to try out these, but even with the very likely rise up in the value of bitcoin, you will not become a millionaire doing this. So, unless you are an ad addict, I would advise you proceed. If you want to try, just Google "totally free bitcoins" or something along those lines and you will find many sites.

Purchasing Bitcoin Hand-to-Hand

Finally, this is going to be the real test of bitcoin. Can people quickly trade them backward and forward? If this can't happen, then there can't actually be a bitcoin economy as merchants will not have the ability to use it. If sellers can't use it, what earthly great is it? Thankfully, this is not actually an issue. iPhone is a little bit of a hold out, but lots of cellular phones have apps (mobile wallets) that will check out QR codes and enable you to send out bitcoin to whomever you really want. You can also show a QR code of your address, and even carry a card in your wallet with your QR code to let people send out bitcoin to you. Depending upon what sort of wallet you have, you can then check to see if the bitcoins have been gotten.

A number of things to keep in mind:

When you established your wallet, if you click around a bit, you will see a choice to pay a charge to speed deals. This cash appears to a bitcoin miner as he/she/they procedure bitcoin info. The miners doing the work of creating blocks of info keeps the system approximately date and protect. The cost is a reward to the miner to be sure to include your info in the next info block and for that reason "confirm" it. In the short-term, miners are making the majority of their cash by mining brand-new coins (check the area on What Are Bitcoins for more details about this). In the long term, as it gets tougher to find brand-new coins, and as the economy increases, the costs will be a reward for miners to keep creating more blocks and keep the economy going. Your wallet ought to be set to pay 0 charges as a default, but if you really want, you can include a charge to prioritize your deals. You are under no commitment to pay a charge, and tons of companies that process tons of little deals (like the ones that pan for gold defined above) produce sufficient costs to keep the miners happy.

In clicking around your wallet, on the deals page or connected to particular deals, you will see a note about verifications. When you make a deal, that info is sent into the network and the network will return a verification that there is no double entry for that bitcoin. It is clever to wait till you get some verifications right before leaving somebody who has paid you. It is actually not really simple to fraud somebody hand-to-hand like this, and it is not really cost-efficient for the criminal, but it can be done.

Where can you purchase bitcoin like this?

You might have a bitcoin Meet up in your location.

You can have a look at localbitcoins.com to find people near you who have an interest in purchasing or selling.

Some are attempting to launch regional street exchanges right across the world. These are called Buttonwoods after the very first street exchange developed on Wall Street in 1792 under a buttonwood tree. See if there is one, or begin one, in your location.

See if you have any good friends who want to try bitcoins out. Actually, the more people who begin using bitcoin, the bigger and more effective it will be come. So please tell 2 good friends.

Some people ask if it is possible to purchase physical bitcoins. The answer to this is both a yes and a no. Bitcoin, by its very nature, is a digital currency and has no physical form. Nevertheless, there are a number of ways in which you can virtually hold a bitcoin in your hands:

Cascascius Coins: These are the creation of Mike Caldwell. He mints physical coins and after that embeds the personal secrets for the bitcoins inside them. You can get the personal key by peeling a hologram from the coin which will then plainly show that the coin has been damaged. Mike has headed out of his way to make sure that he can be relied on. These are a pretty good financial investment technique as in the years to come it might be that these coins are substantial collector's products.

Paper Wallets: A paper wallet just means that instead of keeping the info for your bitcoin kept in a digital wallet, you print the essential info off in addition to a personal key and keep it safe in a safe, in a drawer, or in your bed mattress (if you like). This is highly suggested and cost efficient system for keeping your bitcoin safe. Bear in mind, however, that somebody could take them or if your home burns, they will opt for the home and there will be no other way to get them back. Truly, no different than money. Also, just like Casascius Coins, they will not actually benefit investing till you put them back into the computer system.

There is software application to make printing your paper wallets much easier. bitcoinpaperwallet.com is just one of the best and consists of a really good tutorial about how to use them.

The bitcoins are not actually in the wallet, they are still on the internet. In simple fact, the beyond the wallet will have a QR code that will enable you deliver coins to the wallet at any time you like.

The sealed part of the wallet will have the personal key without which you cannot access the coins. For that reason, only put as tons of coins on the wallet as you want to be unattainable. You will not have the ability to whip this thing out and take out several coins to purchase a cup of coffee. Rather, come up with it as a piggy bank. To get the cash, you need to smash it. It is possible to take out tinier quantities, but at this moment the security of the wallet is jeopardized and it would be simpler for somebody to take the coins. Better to have them all in or out.

People who use paper wallets are normally security mindful, and there are certain methods for the wicked on the planet to hack your computer system. Bitcoinpaperwallet.com gives a ton of great guidance about how to print your wallets firmly.

Some people have also inquired about purchasing bitcoins on eBay. Yes, it is possible, but they will be far overpriced. So, selling on eBay may appear to be a much better alternative given the severe markup over market price you may see. However, similar to anything that is too great to be real, this is too great to be real. As we will clarify in the next area, selling bitcoin that way is just way too dangerous.

How Not to Purchase Bitcoin

In the next area, we are going to clarify a number of bottom lines about purchasing from Bitcoin Exchanges. Right before do, let me give you a caution.

A brief history lesson: When people initially began establishing real company based upon bitcoin, they used all of the tools readily available to any merchant. They sold by charge card and PayPal. The issue with this organisation model was rapidly spotted: bitcoin deals are not reversible by anybody other than the recipient of the cash. Charge card and PayPal have strong purchaser defense policies that make it fairly simple for people to ask for a chargeback. So, wicked people realized this and started making purchases of bitcoin and after that eventually asking for a chargeback. And, since bitcoin is a non-physical item, sent out by brand-new and inadequately comprehended technological ways, the sellers were unable to contest this. Just because of the, sellers stopped accepting charge card and PayPal.

This was a huge issue for the currency: How to move cash between purchasers and seller? Some organisation appeard that would credit you with bitcoin if you wired them cash. Extremely usually these companies would give addresses in Albania, Poland, or Russia. The simple fact is that a lot of these did work and there are a ton of stories on the forums of people who purchased bitcoins that way. But it took a ton of time and in the meantime the purchaser just needed to bite his/her fingernails just wondering if they would get their bitcoins or kiss their financial investment farewell.

Bitcoin ends up being more acceptable and important, we are visiting a variation of the Nigerian Prince rip-off. So the caution is this: we now have exchanges and other services that permit moving cash quickly onto and off of exchanges. Never ever wire cash for bitcoin. It was a temporary, and well-forgotten, moment in the history of bitcoin.

Chapter 7: Where does Bitcoin originate from?

Bitcoin is mined on a dispersed computer system network of users running specialized software application; the network resolves certain mathematical evidence, and look for a specific information series (" block") that produces a specific pattern when the BTC algorithm is applied to it. A match produces a bitcoin. It's intricate and time- and energy-consuming.

Only 21 million bitcoins are ever to be mined (about 11 million are presently in blood circulation). The mathematics problems the network computer systems fix get gradually harder to keep the mining operations and supply in check.

This network also confirms all the deals through cryptography.

How does Bitcoin work?

Web users move digital properties (bits) to one another on a network. There is no online bank; rather, Bitcoin has been referred to as an Internet-wide dispersed journal. Users purchase Bitcoin with money or by selling a service or product for Bitcoin. Bitcoin wallets shop and use this digital currency. Users might sell out of the virtual journal by trading their Bitcoin to somebody else who wants in. Anybody can do this, throughout the world.

There are smart device apps for carrying out mobile Bitcoin deals and Bitcoin exchanges are occupying the Web.

How is Bitcoin valued?

Bitcoin is not held or managed by a banks; it is entirely decentralized. Unlike real-world cash it cannot be cheapened by federal governments or banks.

Instead, Bitcoin's value lies just in its approval between users as a kind of payment and since its supply is limited. Its international currency worths change according to provide and need and market speculation; as more people develop wallets and hold and spend bitcoins, and more organisations accept it, Bitcoin's value will rise up. Banks are now attempting to value Bitcoin and some financial investment sites forecast the cost of a bitcoin will be some thousand dollars in 2014.

What are its advantages?

There are advantages to customers and merchants that want to use this payment choice.

1. Quick deals - Bitcoin is moved quickly online.

2. No fees/low costs-- Unlike charge card, Bitcoin can be used totally free or really low costs. Without the central organization as middle man, there are no permissions (and charges) needed. This enhances earnings margins sales.

3. Gets rid of scams danger -Only the Bitcoin owner can send out payment to the designated recipient, who is the only one who can get it. The network understands the transfer has happened and deals are confirmed; they cannot be challenged or reclaimed. This is huge for online merchants who are usually based on charge card processors' evaluations of whether a deal is deceptive, or organisations that pay the high cost of charge card chargeback.

4. Information is safe and secure-- As we have seen with current hacks on nationwide merchants' payment processing systems, the Web is not always a safe and secure spot for personal information. With Bitcoin, users do not forfeit personal info.

a. They have 2 secrets - a public key that works as the bitcoin address and a personal key with individual information.

b. Deals are "signed" digitally by integrating the general public and personal secrets; a mathematical function is used and a certificate is created showing the user started the deal. Digital signatures are special to each deal and cannot be re-used.

c. The merchant/recipient never ever sees your secret info (name, number, physical address) so it's rather confidential but it is traceable (to the bitcoin address on the general public key).

5. Practical payment system-- Merchants can use Bitcoin totally as a payment system; they do not need to hold any Bitcoin currency since Bitcoin can be converted to dollars. Customers or merchants can sell and out of Bitcoin and other currencies at any time.

6. International payments - Bitcoin is used all over the world; e-commerce merchants and provider can quickly accept global payments, which open the door brand-new prospective markets for them.

7. Easy to track-- The network tracks and completely logs every deal in the Bitcoin block chain (the database). When it comes to possible misbehavior, it is simpler for police authorities to trace these deals.

8. Micropayments are possible - Bitcoins can be split down to one one-hundred-millionth, so running little payments of a dollar or less ends up being a completely free or near-free deal. This could be a genuine advantage for corner store, cafe, and subscription-based sites (videos, publications).

Still a little baffled? Here are several examples of deals:

Bitcoin in the retail environment

At checkout, the payer uses a cell phone app to scan a QR code with all the deal info needed to move the bitcoin to the merchant. Tapping the "Verify" button finishes the deal. If the user does not own any Bitcoin, the network transforms dollars in his account into the digital currency.

The seller can transform that Bitcoin into dollars if it wants to, there were no or extremely low processing costs (rather than 2 to 3 percent), no hackers can take individual customer info, and there is no threat of scams. Really slick.

Bitcoins in hospitality

Hotels can accept Bitcoin for room and dining payments on the properties for visitors who wish to pay by Bitcoin using their mobile wallets, or PC-to-website to pay for an appointment online. A third-party BTC merchant processor can help in managing the deals which it clears over the Bitcoin network. These processing customers are set up on tablets at the facilities' front desk or in the dining establishments for users with BTC cell phone apps. (These payment processors are also readily available for desktops, in retail POS systems, and incorporated into foodservice POS systems.) No charge card or cash really need to change hands.

These cashless deals are quick and the processor can transform bitcoins into currency and make a day-to-day direct deposit into the facility's savings account. It was revealed in January 2014 that 2 Las Vegas hotel-casinos will accept Bitcoin payments at the front desk, in their dining establishments, and in the gift store.

It sounds great - so what's the catch?

Entrepreneur should think about problems of involvement, security and expense.

A reasonably little number of regular customers and merchants presently use or comprehend Bitcoin. Nevertheless, adoption is increasing worldwide and tools and innovations are being developed to make involvement simpler.

It's the Web, so hackers are dangers to the exchanges. The Economic expert reported that a Bitcoin exchange was hacked in September 2013 and $250,000 in bitcoins was taken from users' online vaults. Bitcoins can be taken like other currency, so alert network, server and database security is critical.

Users should thoroughly protect their bitcoin wallets which include their personal secrets. Protected backups or hard copies are essential.

Bitcoin is not controlled or guaranteed by the United States federal government so there is no insurance coverage for your account if the exchange fails or is robbed by hackers.

Bitcoins are fairly pricey. Existing rates and selling costs are readily available on the online exchanges.

The virtual currency is not yet universal but it is getting market awareness and approval. A firm might choose to try Bitcoin to save money on charge card and bank charges, as a consumer benefit, or to see if it helps or prevents sales and success.

Chapter 8: The Best of Bitcoin, the 3 Leading Charting Tools

If you want to be hands-on with your bitcoin financial investment and sell and out of the digital currency to produce a revenue, you will really need the best bitcoin charting tools. In this chapter, you will be introduced to the 3 leading charting platforms you can use to make better financial investment choices when trading bitcoin.

Trading View

Trading View is just one of the most recognized charting tools in the market. It was launched in 2011 as a neighborhood platform where sellers can share their analysis and trading signals. At first, the platform's core focus was on recognized monetary securities and products. Just recently, though, TradingView has added bitcoin and a vast array of other digital currencies to accommodate the rising up need for this brand-new possession class.

Trading View allows users to leverage a range of technical analysis tools to evaluate the cost motions of bitcoin and other possessions. Technical signs like MACD, Bollinger Bands, and the Relative Strength Index can be used to develop technical analysis-based trading methods. Additionally, Trading view allows users to share their trade ideas with one another and discuss them within the platform's social media network.

Coin Tracking

Coin Tracking was launched in 2013 to function as a digital currency financial investment portfolio oversight and management platform. Coin Tracking allows users to monitor all their digital currency financial investments in one spot and supplies a charts and patterns include that enables users to release a variety of technical analysis signs to find patterns for all their preferred digital currencies.

Most likely Coin Tracking's most popular function is the automated generation of tax reports. This is ending up being a significantly essential problem for bitcoin dealers, as tax authorities and monetary regulators are beginning to keep a close eye on digital currency trading activities. The platform's tax reporting function is exceptional for busy dealers who want to make sure that all their digital currency trading activities are effectively reported to the tax man.

Coinigy

Coinigy was launched in 2014 to supply expert digital currency sellers with tools and market information to help them make better financial investment choices. Coinigy not only offers historic and real-time cost information on a wide variety of digital possessions, it also offers exceptional charting tools and links in with some exchanges.

Coinigy enables both banks in addition to individual dealers to deposit funds, monitor their portfolios, examine market patterns, and execute their trades all in one spot.

If you are wanting to actively manage a broad portfolio of digital properties and you choose to do that using only one platform, then Coinigy is your go-to resolution. Coinigy surpasses being a charting tool to offering a one-stop purchase digital currency financiers and is for that reason absolutely worth its relatively high charge.

If you are just aiming to purchase and hold bitcoin, then charting tools will only play a bit part for you and your bitcoin financial investment. Nevertheless, if you want to take an active method to buying bitcoin and other digital properties, then having the right charting tools can make a huge distinction in the long run.

5 Finest Tools To Start Trading Bitcoin

1. Establish trading accounts on the best exchanges

Choosing the right exchanges to trade through can be the distinction between making a ton of cash and losing every little thing.

Coinbase The simplest way to purchase Bitcoin

Coinbase has raised over $100M in endeavor financing from angels and VC s. They re a highly-trusted digital wallet service that permits you to purchase and sell Bitcoin

They make it truly simple for the typical person to start with digital currencies. In simple fact, you can connect your Coinbase account to your bank account and rapidly move cash to and from the exchange.

Bitfinex A really liquid exchange with the capability to brief Bitcoin.

Bitfinex is just one of my preferred spots for shorting Bitcoin. Aside from several technical problems in the past, this exchange is a dependable spot for active sellers.

They regularly rank as one of the leading exchanges by trading volume for the U.S. dollar.

Poloniex The best spot to trade altcoins

Poloniex is a more recent exchange that acquired appeal since they offering margin trading and shorting on lots of the most well-known altcoins.

This is actually the very first began trading Ethereum, and thanks to Poloniex had the ability to catch Ethereum's very first huge booming market.

Bottom line Don't trust exchanges to function as your bank

Look, the reality is that Bitcoin trading is still the Wild West. Some exchanges have been hacked, declared bankruptcy, or actually taken their clients digital currencies.

We can use exchanges to position trades and generate income, but presume the worst. Don't trust them to serve as a checking account. Tons of exchanges are overseas and do not have insurance coverage for you.

2. Use the best charting tools

If you want to be an active trader, then you really need to use the best charting and order execution tools.

The best charting and trade examining tool I ve found is Coinigy.

Coinigy is an all-in-one trading platform that has charting and order execution for all of the crucial digital currencies and exchanges.

You can connect your accounts to Coinigy, actually spot orders, and track your sell a single place.

They have a stunning charting user interface with all the illustration tools and signs you d requirement to evaluate technical analysis.

3. Establish mobile charts & notifies

So it's crucial for me to be able to look at Bitcoin's cost from my cellular phone.

Absolutely no Block is a really easy and effective app that permits you to see an easy cost chart for Bitcoin.

You can also set cost signals in case Bitcoin breaks an important cost level.

4. Move your trading revenues offline into freezer

The most safe spot to keep your digital currencies is in freezer.

Freezer means a wallet that's not linked to the web. This keeps your coins safe from hackers and burglars.

Among my preferred freezer tools is Trezor. This is a hardware Bitcoin wallet that offers supreme security.

There are tons of kinds of cold wallets. It doesn't matter if you use paper wallets, hardware wallets, and even computer system wallets.

Just make certain you comprehend how your Bitcoins are protected and saved!

5. Join a high-value trading community.

The majority of people that try to trade lose cash. There are tons of reasons such a big portion of people lose cash, but the leading reason is an absence of training and education.

Trading is an efficiency activity just like golf, chess, or poker.

And if you do not put in the time to find out the most efficient methods and methods, then chances are you ll lose cash to more proficient sellers.

Once you find out the fundamentals of how to trade Bitcoin, then it's time to join a neighborhood of sellers.

Current & future a figured out of block chain innovation & crypto currency.

Since its creation, Bitcoin has been rather unstable. But based upon its current boom and a projection by Snapchat's very first financier, Jeremy Liew, that it would strike $500,000 by 2030 and the prospect of getting a piece of the Bitcoin pie ends up being much more appealing.

Bitcoin users expect 94% of all bitcoins to be released by 2024. As the number approaches the ceiling of 21 million, tons of expect the earnings miners once made from the creation of brand-new blocks to become so low that they will become minimal. But as more bitcoins go into blood circulation, deal costs could arise and offset this.

When it comes to block chain innovation itself, it has many applications, from banking to the Web of Things. In the next couple of years, BI Intelligence expects businesses to expand their block chain IoT services. Blockchain is an appealing tool that will change parts of the IoT and allow options that offer greater insight into possessions, operations, and supply chains. It will also change how health records and linked medical gadgets shop and transfer information.

Blockchain won't be functional all over, but in a lot of cases, it will belong of the resolution that makes the best usage of the tools in the IoT toolbox. Blockchain can help to resolve specific issues, enhance workflows, and decrease expenses, which are the supreme objectives of any IoT job.

Due to the distinct nature of virtual currencies, there are some intrinsic benefits to negotiating through Bitcoin that users of other currencies do not get. Digital currencies are a reasonably brand-new and untried cash, and users should take care to weigh their advantages and threats. That said, Bitcoin appears to provide some distinct possibilities.

Bitcoin payments are processed through a personal network of computer systems connected through a shared program. Each deal is concurrently made a record of in a "block chain" on each computer system that updates and notifies all accounts.

Bitcoins are either "mined" by a computer system through a procedure of solving significantly intricate mathematical algorithms or acquired with basic nationwide cash currencies and positioned into a "Bitcoin wallet" that is accessed through a cell phone or computer system.

User Privacy.

Bitcoin purchases are discrete. Unless a user willingly releases his Bitcoin deals, his purchases are never ever connected with his individuality, similar to cash-only purchases, and cannot be traced back to him. In simple fact, the confidential Bitcoin address that is produced for user purchases changes with each deal.

No Third-party Disruptions.

Among the most commonly advertised advantages of Bitcoin is that federal governments, banks and other monetary intermediaries have no other way to disrupt user deals or spot freezes on Bitcoin accounts. The system is simply peer-to-peer; users experience a higher degree of liberty than with nationwide currencies.

Purchases Are Not Taxed.

Since there is no chance for 3rd parties to determine, track or obstruct deals that are denominated in Bitcoins, among the significant benefits of Bitcoin is that sales taxes are not added onto any purchases.

Really Low Deal Costs.

Requirement wire transfers and foreign purchases usually include costs and exchange expenses. Since Bitcoin deals have no intermediary organizations or federal government participation, the expenses of negotiating are kept really low. This can be a major benefit for tourists. In addition, any transfer in Bitcoins happens really rapidly, removing the hassle of common permission requirements and wait durations.

Mobile Payments

Like with tons of online payment systems, Bitcoin users can pay for their coins anywhere they have Web access. This means that buyers never ever need to travel to a bank or a shop to purchase an item. Nevertheless, in contrast to online payments made with U.S. savings account or charge card, individual info is not needed to finish any deal.

How bitcoin, Ethereum, and the other significant cryptocurrencies compare to one another

Unless you ve been hiding under a rock, you re most likely conscious that we re in the middle of a cryptocurrency blasts. In one year, the value of all currencies increased an incredible 1,466% and more recent coins like Ethereum have even signed up with Bitcoin in acquiring some mainstream approval.

Nevertheless, even with the enjoyment and action that includes the space, a major issue still exists for the layperson: it's actually challenging to figure out the distinctions between cryptocurrencies like Bitcoin, Ethereum, Ethereum Classic, Litecoin, Ripple, and Dash.

For this reason, we dealt with social trading network eToro to come up with an infographic that breaks down the significant distinctions between these coins all in one spot.

Chapter 10: Information about Altcoins

A description of significant coins

Here are descriptions of the significant cryptocurrencies, that make up 84% of the coin universe.

Bitcoin

Bitcoin is the initial cryptocurrency, and was released as open-source software application in 2009. Utilizing a brand-new dispersed journal referred to as the blockchain, the Bitcoin procedure enables users to make peer-to-peer deals using digital currency while keeping away from the double costs issue.

No main authority or server confirms deals, and instead the authenticity of a payment is determined by the decentralized network itself.

Bottom Line: Bitcoin is the initial cryptocurrency with the most liquidity and substantial network impacts. It also has brand acknowledgment around the globe, with an eight-year performance history.

Litecoin

Lite coin was launched in 2011 as an early option to Bitcoin. Around this time, progressively specialized and pricey hardware was needed to mine bitcoins, making it tough for routine people to participate the action. Litecoin's algorithm was an effort to even the playing field so that anybody with a routine computer system could participate in the network.

Bottom Line: Other altcoins have removed some of Litecoin's market share, but it still has an early mover benefit and some strong network results.

Ripple

Ripple is substantially different from Bitcoin. That's as Ripple is basically a worldwide settlement network for other currencies just like USD, Bitcoin, EUR, GBP, or any other systems of value (i.e. regular flier miles, products).

To make any such a settlement, though, a small cost must be paid in XRP (Ripple's native tokens) and these are what trade on crypt currency markets.

Bottom Line: Ripple works on a lot of the exact same concepts of Bitcoin, but for a various purpose: to act as the intermediary for all worldwide FX deals. If it can effectively catch that market, the potential is high.

Ethereum

Ethereum is an open software application platform based upon block chain innovation that allows designers to build and release decentralized applications.

In the Ethereum block chain, rather than mining for bitcoin, miners work to make ether, a kind of crypto token that fuels the network. Beyond a tradable crypt currency, ether is also used by application designers to pay for deal costs and services on the Ethereum network.

Bottom Line: Ethereum serves a various purpose than other cryptocurrencies, but it has rapidly grown to displace all but Bitcoin in value. Some specialists are so bullish on Ethereum that they even see it ending up being the world's leading crypto currency in just a brief period of time but only time will tell.

Ethereum Classic

In 2016, the Ethereum community dealt with a hard choice: The DAO, an equity capital firm built on top of the Ethereum platform, had $50 million in ether taken from it through a security vulnerability.

Most of the Ethereum community chose to help The DAO by tough forking the currency, and after that changing the block chain to return the taken earnings back to The DAO. The minority thought this idea breached the crucial structure of immutability that the blockchain was created around, and kept the initial Ethereum block chain the way it was. Thus, the Traditional label.

Bottom Line: As time goes on, Ethereum Classic has been taking a different identity from its larger brother or sister. With comparable abilities and a various set of concepts, Ethereum Classic could still have upside.

Dash

Dash is an effort to enhance on Bitcoin in 2 primary regions: speed of deals, and privacy. To do this, it has two-tier architecture with miners and also master nodes that help the network perform sophisticated functions like near-instant deals and coin-mixing to offer extra personal privacy.

Bottom Line: The developments behind Dash are intriguing, and could help to make the coin more consumer-friendly than other options.

Coinbase vs. Blockchain: Last Ideas

In using both services, it's clear that each has its own advantages, depending upon your own intent for usage. You can use either to get BTC or ETH or use a mobile app for benefit. Nevertheless, it is very likely much easier for beginner to ready up on the user-friendly Coinbase platform. If you re only planning to use crypt currency deals without the requirement for a bank, Blockchain is your flawless wallet.

What You Should Know Just Before You Start Trading Cryptocurrency

There are just a couple of things to know about trading cryptocurrency beyond what was kept in mind above. Below are a few of the most essential things to know right before beginning:

A cryptocurrency exchange is not part of the routine stock market. Beneath we will suggest using an exchange/broker Coinbase, but you can also use the associated GDAX (the pro variation of Coinbase with lower costs). Neither of these is the exact same as Wall Street and its exchanges (exact same general mechanics, different specifics, and different entities).

A newbie may choose to trade cryptocurrency stocks on the stock exchange (GBTC is a trust that owns Bitcoin and sells shares of it; trading this keeps away from you needing to trade cryptocurrency straight). The primary Bitcoin stock here in 2018 is GBTC. Know that GBTC trades at a premium (meaning bitcoins are less expensive than purchasing shares of the GBTC trust), which isn't suitable. Also, cryptocurrency trading is a 24-hour market, where the conventional stock exchange is not. Discover more about the GBTC Bitcoin Trust and the associated advantages and disadvantages right before you invest.

Believe the easiest spot to purchase, sell, and shop coins is Coinbase (and our tutorial below will help you ready up with that), but you can only purchase, sell, and shop Bitcoin, Ethereum, Litecoin, and Bitcoin Money on Coinbase. If you are serious about trading cryptocurrency, you ll need another exchange like Coinbase's GDAX, Bittrex, Binance, or Kraken (and you ll very likely want to find a wallet to keep your coins in). See a leading 5 list of cryptocurrency exchanges and the very best Bitcoin Exchanges ranked (those above are my choices).

The cryptocurrency market is remarkably unpredictable in 2018. You can succeed in a minute and lose it in the next whether you trade Bitcoin, another coin, or the GBTC Bitcoin trust. Think about reducing threats, hedging, and not going long with all your investable funds.

SUGGESTION: If you trade only the leading coins by market cap (that is coins like Bitcoin Ethereum), or GBTC, then the chances of losing every little thing over night are slim (possible, but slim). Other cryptocurrencies are riskier (but can provide fast gains on a pretty good day).

SUGGESTION: There are several sides to cryptocurrency. 1. you can trade and purchase it, 2. you can use it for deals (anywhere a coin type is accepted), 3. you can break out a graphics processing system and some software application and mine coins (see how to mine coins). Those are all legitimate and intriguing, but with that in mind, this page is concentrated on trading cryptocurrency (and for that reason also buying it).

With that said, even if you want to do the other things with cryptocurrencies, you still really need to be established for trading.

On cryptocurrency mining: As kept in mind, one way to buy cryptocurrency is through cryptocurrency mining. That is a legitimate way to begin investing if say you really love computer system video gaming and really need a brand-new rig and want to buy percentages of cryptocurrency while perhaps making back some of the expense of the rig (and perhaps even recovering cost) but that is a completely different topic. The typical financier will want to trade USD for cryptocurrency on an exchange and keep away from the intricacies and financial investments of mining. In all cases, unless you already have a pretty good rig with a great graphics card, you ll really need to put down USD in advance anyhow.

What You Required to Know to Start Trading Cryptocurrency

For those who want to trade crypto currency regardless of the above notes:

A newbie ought to begin by picking a business with a really good credibility that offers an exchange and wallet (to help keep the procedure simple).

A newbie must also begin by trading popular coins. Presently, in 2018, we are describing coins like Bitcoin (BTC) and Ethereum (ETH). In the future, this could change.

Since the above holds true, a pretty good start for any American wanting to trade crypto currency is beginning with Coinbase.com (the most well-known crypto currency site in America, and a service that offers a single platform for a Bitcoin wallet, Ethereum wallet, Litecoin wallet, Bitcoin Money wallet, and a currency exchange).

After you master Coinbase, then you are prepared for say GDAX and other exchanges like Bittrex, Binance, or Kraken.

IDEA: A very good very first venture into crypto currency investing is the apparent, purchasing a major crypto currency like Bitcoin. After that, you ll most likely want to trade USD for crypto on an exchange like GDAX. Once you have done that, you could try trading BTC and ETH for other cryptocurrencies. Trading crypto sets can be gratifying, but it is more intricate and usually more dangerous than just purchasing a single crypto currency as a financial investment.

IDEA: Do refrain from doing margin trading unless you know precisely what that is and are a professional. Cryptocurrency is unpredictable; you can wind up losing all your cash in an immediate if you aren't mindful.

IDEA: If you do not comprehend the tax ramifications of trading crypto currency tread really thoroughly. There are some nasty traps you could fall into when trading coins. For one, they are not always thought about like-kind possessions. If that is complicated, then think about sticking to trading USD for coins in Coinbase till you comprehend the idea.

How to Shop Your Bitcoin as Safely as Possible

How do Bitcoin Wallets Work?

The crucial thing to comprehend is that no matter what you do, you won't actually be saving the bitcoin itself. That's as a bitcoin isn't an item, it's an encrypted address on the block chain. What you own is a special key that opens a particular bitcoin area, and that's what you really need to be securing at all times by keeping it in a wallet.

With that covered, there are several different methods to keep your bitcoin depending upon how safe and secure you want to be and how much you prepare to use it regularly.

Why You Need To Use a Hardware Wallet

The much easier way to keep your bitcoin and other crypto currency is in a digital wallet online or in your area on your Smart device or computer system. But leaving your bitcoin in public view can open you as much as attacks from hackers and phishing frauds. That's why the best alternative is a hardware wallet that shops your bitcoin offline.

Many hardware wallets appear like USB drives and can be quickly linked to a computer system. They use a PIN number for security, in addition to a secondary password called a seed in case you forget the PIN. If you forget both passwords you re practically screwed, so it may be worth writing the seed down someplace safe offline.

The other largest downside to a hardware wallet is that if you lose it you can't recuperate the bitcoin. So ensure to develop at least one backup on another encrypted storage gadget.

Other Choices

Another problem with hardware wallets is that they can make the procedure of actually investing your bitcoin a lot harder. The best resolution is to keep a percentage of bitcoin in a digital wallet like Mycelium Wallet, that's created to work well with offline storage gadgets.

Finally, if you want to keep your bitcoin offline but do not want to handle a hardware wallet, you may want to think about a paper wallet instead. This is actually just a notepad with your public and personal secrets printed on it, which can be used to access your bitcoin.

If you do not intend on touching your bitcoin for a while then a paper wallet is a really good choice. Just ensure you put your paper wallet someplace really safe and after that do not forget where it is.

Chapter 11: How to Keep Your Cryptocurrency Safe and Secure

Preferred characteristics of a Cryptocurrency Wallet

What are the preferred qualities of a crypto wallet and how tough can choose a wallet to be? This relatively simple answer, regrettably, doesn't have a gratifying answer: benefit might come at the expense of security; extra functions might come at the expense of a steeper knowing curve. More importantly, what are the characteristics that, eventually, you value over the other ones? See the list beneath, not in order of significance:

Expense. Is it totally free? What are the disadvantages of using this wallet?

Security. Does the business have a performance history of security quality?

Movement. Is it simple to keep and challenging to lose? Is it available anytime, anywhere?

User-friendliness. Is the wallet UI intuitively developed? Can I save a series of altcoins?

Benefit. Am I able to make a quick purchase when the time requires it?

Style. Do I have a weak point for cool tech gizmos?

You might really want a wallet that offers the best mix of those qualities. Keep in mind, all wallets have their edges and drawbacks.

7 Should Have Wallets: How To Keep Your Cryptocurrency Safe

Keep Key Hardware Wallet

The coolest looking tech gizmo to display to your good friends. Made by a reasonably brand-new business, Keep Key offers a hardware wallet of a sleek design. KeepKey is said to be a port of Trezor's code and firmware, so their primary distinction is the product. KeepKey feels a bit like a premium wallet but may be a little on the heavy side and for this reason more vulnerable to drops. It features a requirement, easy to use customer UI.

Nano Journal's Hardware Wallet

Nano Journal's is just as protected as the other 2 hardware wallets. It is well-known just because of its reasonably low cost of $65 compared to its rivals. Being tinier than KeepKey, it is more portable and simpler to carry around. It is a hardware wallet that comes at a really competitive cost.

Trezor Hardware Wallet

Trezor is just one of the very first movers in the hardware wallet market and sets the gold requirement for crypto security. Trezor has a credibility for supplying superior security, securing against both virtual and physical theft. What Trezor does not have in style, it more than comprises in the security department. Even if your PC is jeopardized with malware, your personal secrets will still be safe with Trezor. In this sense, Trezor is more of a vault than a wallet.

Coinbase Hot Wallet

Coinbase is an online web-based wallet and is the beginner-friendly variation of GDAX. As a hot wallet, you can quickly move to the GDAX exchange quickly, and totally free. In the exact same user interface, you can make fast purchases with fiat. What's more, 100% of your crypto holdings on Coinbase is guaranteed. You can trigger 2-Step Confirmation and Google Authenticator for more defense, and Coinbase even has a vault readily available if you wish to trade benefit for an included layer of security. The only disadvantage is that Coinbase only offers Bitcoin and Ethereum wallets.

MyEtherWallet Paper Wallet

Paper wallets are for those who wish to have their own personal wallets without handing over money for hardware wallets. The cash saved could be bought their coins. Just produce your wallet online at myetherwallet.com and note your personal secrets. The site doesn't shop or transfer any of your personal info. If you do not trust the online variation, you can even download it from GitHub and run it offline. Paper wallets are completely free but need an extensive knowledge to set it up effectively. Simply put, this kind of wallets typically take a ton of trouble and are not advised for amateurs.

Jaxx Software Application Wallet

Carrying your crypto around securely and easily is no longer a far-off dream. Behold Jaxx, the world's very first mobile wallet resolution. Variations for iOS, android, desktop and web browser are now readily available. Jaxx uses a mnemonic seed to back your wallet or move it to a various gadget. Jaxx permits you to get your funds, scan QR code, see your crypto holdings, all in one instinctive app. Advanced functions like shape shift incorporation and several platforms wallet linkage makes this the chosen wallet for the tech savvy. The only downside with this wallet is that it may have a high knowing curve, and functions may not be steady with all the brand-new combinations. With time, this will prove to be an appealing resolution.

Electrum Software Application Wallet

Electrum is a quick, light-weight wallet for desktop and mobile users. It has a long list of supported functions to make it the most versatile wallet today. It offers freezer options, incorporation with hardware wallets (Keep Key, Nano Journal S, Trezor) and able to attain privacy (with Tor). On the security side, Electrum allows multi-sig assistance, and it is not connected to a central server, so server downtime will not be a concern. In general, Electrum is the recognized software application wallet resolution out there that warrants a try-out.

Chapter 12: Errors to Keep Away from When Trading

Refraining from doing own research

Don't go to one forum or on social networks platforms, listen to what couple of people are saying and after that make a trading choice.

You need to do an in-depth research right before making any relocation. Check out charts. Recognize resistant zones and assistance zones to comprehend the existing cost.

Discover to check out pattern lines on Candlestick chart to know when the cost will decrease and when up.

If all of these sound a little complex then the least you can do is collect around the news from several sources and after that examine yourself which sources are more dependable and certain. (Ensure the news resources are reliable though.).

NEVER listen to a single person or source. Listen to everybody and after that make your own choice by taking a look at the present cost movement.

Panic Purchasing and Panic Selling.

This is the most typical error amongst the novices. When they do not know how market functions and how cost relocations and they have invested cash that they cannot afford to lose they always wind up panic selling.

Just when they see the cost falling even a bit, most of them wind up selling their Bitcoin even when it means costing loss.

They just want to save whatever cash they can, understanding less, the cost routinely goes up and down. And sometimes, the down is even larger as a result of some unexpected news. But at the end, it always will return to typical back on track to climb up higher.

Likewise, when newbies see Bitcoin cost rising up, they stress purchase, investing all their cash in one go without doing any research. They hope that cost will keep increasing. But this doesn't always show up well. The cost can decrease anytime.

(Naturally, panic purchasing doesn't hurt in the long run. As the cost will always rise up at the end. But you do lose out chances to make more cash from trading.).

Investing all your cash in single purchase.

Do not spend all your cash in a single purchase. Even when you have found the right entry point, you believe the cost has bottomed out and the Bull Run is only a matter of time now, do not spend all your cash in one go.

Since forecasting Bitcoin market is unrealistic. What if after you have spent all the cash, cost drops farther? You would get into a total loss without any more cash at hand to leverage this low cost.

In the exact same way, if cost continues going up, you can spend the cash you have, in little pieces, and make a good revenue, rather than investing simultaneously.

Keep in mind, trading is not practically making huge cash. It's also about reducing threats.

Not setting stop-loss and take-profit positions.

Various sellers have different limits for risk-taking. After a point, it may not be affordable for you to take the loss. Also, after you have got the amount of revenue that you had prepare for, it may not be a great idea to continue and run the risk of the fall of cost.

To counter both the circumstances, you should set stop-loss and take-profit positions. Meaning, you should know at what point you should leave the trade when you re losing cash and when you have made sufficient earnings.

This relocation helps you decrease the threat included without jeopardizing in your monetary objectives.

Trading with feelings.

Never ever trade with feelings. It's an crucial rule of trading in any instrument, be it Bitcoin or stock.

Keep all your feelings at bay and make choices realistically. Don't get too connected to your holding. Comprehend that huge Bitcoin cost movement is rather typical. Some days are bad, some are great. Always depend on your reasoning and analysis when making purchasing and selling choice. Never ever go I just feel like.

Generally, psychological trading will bring you loss or stop you from making more earnings.

Ending up being too greedy.

When the cost is going up, rather than leaving at the correct time after we have made a pretty good earnings, we continue with the flow, wishing to make more earnings.

Never ever be too greedy. Constantly know when to take out your earnings, leave the game and delight in the program. Keep in mind, when the cost is going up too quick prematurely, a correction is always originating from behind.

So, it is always a really good choice to make an exit right before the correction, dip comes. When you re acting greedy, not only are you running the risk of the present revenues, you re also denying yourself of the chances to make more cash when the cost decreases.

So, stop acting greedily. Always have an exit strategy.

Chapter 13: How to Sell It

Squandering your Bitcoins is not as direct as purchasing them. If you choose to sell your Bitcoins online, you can either do it through an exchange, direct trade or perform a peer-to-peer deal.

Beyond the convenience of your own home, you can withdraw flat cash using a Bitcoin ATM or sell your Bitcoins personally.

Exchanges.

In spite of having some disadvantages, exchanges are a one-stop resolution when it pertains to trading Bitcoins. When it comes to selling the cryptocurrency, exchanges serve as an intermediary that holds both seller's and purchaser's funds.

First, you really need to establish an account with an exchange of your choice. The outright bulk of reliable exchanges will need complete identity confirmation and a linked checking account so that you can withdraw your funds.

Then, you just merely position a sell offer, specifying the kind of currency you wish to trade, its amount and your asking cost per system. The exchange will immediately finish the deal once somebody matches your offer.

After the funds are credited to your account, you will really need to withdraw them to your linked savings account. This can in some cases take an extreme amount of time, particularly if the exchange is experiencing concerns with its banks or dealing with liquidity issues. Some months right before its personal bankruptcy, the Mt. Gox exchange was experiencing this precise issue. Additionally, some banks just outright refuse to process deals with funds gotten through cryptocurrency trading.

It is also essential to think about a charge you ll really need to pay to use some exchanges. For instance, among the world's largest cryptocurrency exchanges CEX.io charges a flat cost of $50 for withdrawal through Bank transfer, $3.80 if you re withdrawing your funds to a Visa card and 1.2 percent of a deal + $3.80 if you re using MasterCard. The withdrawal costs can differ significantly depending upon an exchange, but deal charges are often either small or non-existent at all.

In addition, a lot of exchanges will have a limitation on the amount of cash you re enabled to shop. The limitation will increase in time if you stay faithful to a specific exchange.

Finally, it is very important to bear in mind that in spite of offering wallet services, exchanges are by no means a protected and trustworthy spot to keep your funds. They are really susceptible to hacker attacks, and there have also been circumstances of exchanges closing down and running away with their users funds. For this reason why you should take full obligation for your own funds and save any amount that is not instantly needed in a safe and secure offline wallet.

Direct trades for selling bitcoins.

This service is available on sites typically related to exchanges and consists of an intermediary assisting in the connection.

First, you will really need to sign up as a seller. Apart from establishing your profile, you will really need to totally validate your identity. Once you re signed up, you can publish a deal suggesting your objective to sell some Bitcoins. When a purchaser wants to trade with you, you get an alert from the service and after that you are only communicating with the purchaser. The site simply works as a platform to finish the trade.

The procedure of selling Bitcoins on some of those sites can be rather included and lengthy. So, it is necessary to do your research right before picking a trading platform and ensure you have the time and persistence needed.

Some of the sites offering the alternative of direct trading are BitBargain, Bittylicious, Coinbase, Openbitcoins, Bitsquare and LocalBitcoins.

ELEMENTS IMPACTING THE RATE OF BITCOIN.

1) Animal spirits.

Economic experts have long had an idea that psychological aspects impact financier choices. This is called animal spirits and describes financiers making choices based upon the conduct of other market individuals and their own instincts, instead of tough analysis.

Analysis of the cost of Bitcoin shows that positive media coverage is just one of the primary aspects driving the cost.

Positive media coverage of brand-new innovations triggers a widely known hype-cycle a peak of buzz is followed by a trough of disillusionment.

This was most obvious in the early days of Bitcoin, when traditional press began to report on the brand-new currency and triggered certain brief cost spikes and collapses. As media coverage boosts and other aspects are taken in, it is tougher to distil the influence of the media alone.

2) Political danger.

Political threat around nationwide currencies might also impact the cost of Bitcoin as people use it to move against cost motions in a specific currency, or they really need to rapidly move big quantities of value out a nation or currency.

The recession in Greece in 2015 was followed by reports of increased purchasing of Bitcoin by Greek people wanting to secure their wealth. This did not appear to impact the cost of Bitcoin on international markets, though, which stayed stable between A$ 300 and $400 for the majority of that year.

But uneasiness about the nationwide referendum for Britain to leave the European Union (Brexit) on June 23 2016 did result in a boost in the cost of Bitcoin together with a decline in the value of the British pound.

The pound began dropping around Might 20 2016. By July 25 it was more than 10% beneath its pre-Brexit value. For the exact same duration the cost of Bitcoin increased by over 65% (from £ 302 to £ 502).

The election of Donald Trump as United States president was also followed by 2 months of high rises up in the cost of Bitcoin. Tons of associated this to unpredictability in the United States economy.

3) Regulative relocations.

Regulators worldwide have needed to reach the development of Bitcoin. They need to choose, for example, how it will be dealt with by the tax system, or whether and what policy definitely applies to its usage.

2 events in specific emphasize the effect guidelines can have on the cost.

The statement that Bitcoin would be thought about legal tender in Japan pushed the cost of Bitcoin up by 2% in just 24 hr, and increased the cost internationally by 160% for the next 2 months.

China's choice to close down some Bitcoin exchanges and restriction preliminary coin offerings (a type of crowdfunding usually paid for with cryptocurrencies) sent out the cost of Bitcoin dropping by 29% in 24 hr.

When is the correct time to purchase bitcoin?

Similar to any market, absolutely nothing is for sure.

Throughout its history, Bitcoin has typically increased in value at a really fast lane, followed by a sluggish, consistent failure till it supports.

Usage tools like Bitcoin Knowledge or Cryptowatch to examine charts and comprehend Bitcoin's cost history.

Bitcoin is worldwide and not impacted by any single nation's monetary circumstances or stability.

For instance, speculation about the Chinese Yuan devaluating has, in the past, triggered more need from China, which also brought up the currency exchange rate on U.S. and Europe based exchanges.

Worldwide turmoil is typically viewed as advantageous to Bitcoin's cost since Bitcoin is apolitical and sits outside the control or impact of any particle federal government.

When thinking of how economics and politics will impact Bitcoin's cost, it's essential to believe on a worldwide scale and not almost what's going on in a single nation.

Sites to Purchase and Sell Bitcoin and Other Cryptocurrencies

Coinbase

When you use Coinbase, you are going to have the ability to automate the purchase of your bitcoins for every single week or monthly. It's a pretty simple platform to use whenever you re just starting out with bitcoin trading. Nevertheless, if you are going to be carrying out any suspicious activities that are in the gray zone of bitcoins, then you may want to keep an eye out for this site as they are quite stringent about their policies. The business that runs Coinbase is extremely specific about what types of activities can happen on this exchange.

Kraken

Kraken is a bitcoin provider that's totallyengrossed on trading of bitcoins. You will have the ability to manage and brief on the platform, and that makes it a great choice for a ton of bitcoin dealers out there. If you re anxious about the authenticity of the platform, do not concern! Kraken is among the very first bitcoin exchanges to clear a self-governing audit, which means that your deals are totally safe on this site. If you are a trader of Bitcoin, then this one is absolutely one that you ve got to take a look at.

Nevertheless, when you use Kraken you have got to keep in mind just one thing. You are going to need to establish 2FA (2-factor authentication) in order for your account to be kept up on the site. Without that, your whole account will be erased and drained, so beware!

BitStamp

BitStamp is the very first certified operator of Bitcoin. With this exchange, you are going to have the ability to use your credit or debit card to do bitcoin exchanges, which is a big plus for a lot of purchasers and sellers out there. Another truly substantial benefit that features BitStamp is the simple fact that you can take out your bitcoins for real, physical gold! That's right, you re going to have the ability to take out your bitcoinsand get real gold in return. That's flawless for those of you who enjoy keeping gold around for the rough financial times we may strike.

LocalBitcoins

LocalBitcoins enables those who sell bitcoins to get in touch with those people who purchase bitcoins. Once you log onto this site, the next step will result in a page that's particular to your nation, which allows you to select who you re going to purchase or sell your bitcoins from. There's an integrated escrow system, which is great for defense to guarantee that you get your payment.

This is the best system for those of you who choose dealing with people, instead of through a big business. The downside that features using this platform is the simple fact that fraudsters can quickly get on there and draw you in. You certainly do not want to get associated with a phony banking deal, so ensure that you take care when using this platform.

While bitcoins might seem like the currency of the future but the tax future of bitcoins is definitely unsure. Being virtual currency they are challenging to represent and it is rather a job to transform their ever-changing worths in regards to cash. However, if one idea changed the way deals happen, another fantastic one may offer a resolution for this too

ItBit

With this choice, note that you re going to need to pay a little charge to become a part of itBit. There are quite good rates for the bitcoins, but that charge is going to make it a bit more pricey than it would be otherwise, which is great to bear in mind while you re trading. Nevertheless, another essential thing to keep in mind about this platform is that there are exceptional services readily available to those of you who are selling a great deal of bitcoins.

OKCoin

OKCoin flawless for both purchasers and sellers of Bitcoin. You only get the nuts and
bolts with this site. There are no fancy logo designs and cool results, which is good to a
degree. It's a really useful site to use, so it won't take wish for you to get used to using
it. Nevertheless, it's still a much better and simpler platform for those of you who are
used to trading you ll have the ability to pick up faster than an amateur.

BTC-e

The best feature of BTC-e is the simple fact that it is extremely transparent. You ll see
the existing cost of the bitcoin at every moment you re on the site and all of the current
deals, which is a great function to have in a bitcoin exchange. Another great thing that
features this site is the chat box function, which can help you out with valuable
suggestions whenever you re trading.

PROS

No tax

There are no taxes included with bitcoin. This should be music to many individuals. No requirement to pay extra taxes on your purchases.

High degree of personal privacy

Practically all bitcoin deals are very protected and really personal. Users of bitcoin usage pseudonyms for their deals. This high degree of personal privacy makes using bitcoin really interesting lots of people.

Low deal charges

Costs charged by online payment processors can be high if the volume is high. Lots of merchants might balk at the costs and exchange expenses gradually. Because bitcoin is not managed, it has really low costs and it's still safe and secure since it doesn't count on one point of failure as prevails with typical payment processors.

It's also much quicker since there is no approval procedure or confirmation needed as bitcoin is exceptionally personal.

Bitcoin is deflationary

Among the special functions of bitcoin is that only 21 million bitcoins will be created. That is the limitation. That means the value of the coins will grow in time.

Easy to use

Bitcoin was produced for the web and it's just a dream to use. To send out bitcoin to somebody, all you will need to do is type in the receiver's address and send out. It's as quickly as sending out an e-mail. No trouble. No waiting times. A very versatile form of online payment.

Bitcoin is not controlled

That means there are no banks or banks controlling bitcoin to get their own program. Bitcoin gets rid of all 3rd party disturbance in the deals. No one can freeze a bitcoin account.

Conventional cash depends on trust. The people really need to rely on the banks that they position their cash in. With the collapse of banks, dodgy practices, works on the bank, and so on lots of people have despaired in banks and actually see these organizations as damaging to society in general.

CONS

Bitcoin needs some knowing

There is a finding out curve included when it pertains to bitcoin. Unlike standard cash that we are accustomed to using from an early age, bitcoin is reasonably brand-new. The idea needs some research study and understanding.

There are very few extensive guides on the topic. Users will really need to comprehend the terms like block chain, cryptography, mining, and so on. All these can be found out by utilizing Google. If you really wish to comprehend bitcoin, there is sufficient info online to make you skilled on the topic.

Declined in a lot of spots

Unlike PayPal which has been commonly adopted, many merchants have not begun accepting bitcoin as a method of payment yet. So, if you re a purchaser, you might not have the ability to make buy from a lot of spots.

Tough to acquire

In the start, it was fairly simple to mine for bitcoin. Now, as the number gets higher, it is getting exceptionally hard to acquire bitcoin. The good news is, there are more bitcoin exchanges opening with more prepared sellers.

Bitcoin deal can be sluggish sometimes

The majority of bitcoin deals are quick but since this a peer to peer system, there is a time set for verification on the deal. The larger the deal, the longer the wait. You can choose no verifications and not need to wait as long but it would be a good idea to wait.

Bitcoin can be taken

Although bitcoin is a digital currency, it can still be taken. Lots of bitcoin owners keep their information in digital drives and protect these drives in security deposits to guarantee they re not taken. You will have a digital wallet to safeguard your bitcoin but you need to know how to do it properly.

Bitcoin Wallets Can Be Lost

If a hard disk crashes, or an infection damages information, and the wallet file is damaged, Bitcoins have basically been lost. There is absolutely nothing that can done to recuperate it. These coins will be forever and ever orphaned in the system. This can bankrupt a rich Bitcoin financier within seconds without any way form of healing. The coins the financier owned will also be completely orphaned.

No Physical Form

Since Bitcoins do not have a physical form, it cannot be used in physical shops. It would always need to be converted to other currencies. Cards with Bitcoin wallet info saved in them have been proposed, but there is no agreement on a specific system. Since there would be several contending systems, merchants would find it impractical to support all Bitcoin cards, and for that reason users would be pushed to transform Bitcoins anyhow, unless a universal system is proposed and executed.

Chapter 15: Calculators to Take into Account

Whether you want to examine historical bitcoin returns, compute possible bitcoin mining success, or just learn how much bitcoin you can purchase for $10,000, there are free-to-use online calculators that cover all these functions. Here are the best.

Most likely the most crucial bitcoin calculator you will use as a financier in bitcoin is a bitcoin currency conversion calculator. This calculator enables you to check how much bitcoin is presently worth in dollars or other standard currencies.

A user-friendly online calculator that permits you to transform any fiat currency amount into its bitcoin equivalent and vice versa is the bitcoin currency conversion calculator by GoBitcoin.io.

For instance, using this calculator you can discover much $1,000 is definitely worth in bitcoin at its existing market rate. The marketplace rates you can select from are from Coinbase, Bitstamp, and the Coindesk BPI.

You can also do this estimation for all significant global currencies, which is why this calculator is preferred amongst global bitcoin users.

Finest Bitcoin Mining Success Calculator

If you are thinking about venturing into bitcoin mining, you should initially make use of a bitcoin mining success calculator to get an idea of how lucrative such an endeavor could be.

The contrast platform CryptoCompare has among the most easy to use bitcoin mining success calculators that can show you how much earnings you would create from mining bitcoin given the amount of mining power you have and the electrical energy costs you would sustain.

While this calculator can give you a rough quote of how much earnings you could produce, remember that the mining problem, along with the cost of bitcoin, can vary rather considerably, which will impact your real mining success. For that reason, revenue figures from bitcoin mining success calculators can only be used as assistance and are not set in stone.

Finest Bitcoin Historic Return Calculator

If you want to evaluate historical bitcoin returns, the best calculator you can use is the Bitcoin Inflated Adjusted Return Calculator by the individual financing platform DQYDJ. This calculator lets you calculate the typical annualized earnings bitcoin has created for any given period since September 2010. It also enables you to change the returns for inflation to offer you with the real roi of holding bitcoin.

Additionally, you can also use the Financial investment Returns Calculator by the Bitcoin Retirement Mutual fund company BitcoinIRA, which enables you to determine how much a financial investment in bitcoin, would be well worth today for any given year from 2012 onward.

While historical returns are by no means a warranty for future returns, they can give some assistance on possible predicted returns, which can be helpful when building a broad, varied portfolio of properties.

Making use of this currency provoked nations like Japan to leap in to the current of BTC. This year at least 250,000 shops in are expected to get such lawful deals in June or July. Mexico is just one of the nations in Latam that has seen a location of chance in this sector.

Bitso, the Mexican business is a great example of the. At the end of 2016 it had caught about 30,000 brand-new consumers, just in 27 months. 20,000 Of them, had signed up with the business in the last quarter of that year. While Donald Trump was crowned as President of the United States and the Ford automobile plant deserted his task in the Mexican state of San Luis Potosi, Bitso had a great day and nor the political neither the financial environment impacted it at all, in contrast to other currencies.

The marketplace so-called criptocurrencies or criptocoins is less susceptible to cyber-attacks, in contrast to Dollar or Euro, which just recently were impacted by the WannaCry infection, a computer system worm that supervised of securing the files on a computer system and requiring a ransom payment right before enabling access to them again.

The future of bitcoin depends on that sort of dilemma, as it shows the dependability of innovation and spots development as a location of chance and development for the monetary world, which in the last few years has found greater penetration through digital platforms and electronic payment techniques, for example, in spots communication and success of conventional financial systems is managed.

Bitcoin's Future Dispute

There's a long way to go before Bitcoin ends up being an internationally accepted form of currency, virtual or not, with some counties having actually outright prohibited using Bitcoin, though the number of nations are reducing, with the larger problem being the absence of policy on Bitcoin itself paired with issues over innovation restrictions.

Technological development over the brief to medium-term will definitely affect the value of the marketplaces and, as an international regulative landscape develops, we would expect the use and need to increase, driving the value, the kinds of returns that are not obvious with money, still presently keeping its Money is King status.

Whether financiers think about Bitcoin as an alternative hedge or a financial investment remains to be seen. In either case, when thinking about the year-on-year rise in the value of Bitcoin, just shy of 200%, the only way is up should regulative walls continue to fall and deal volumes continue to arise, with Bitcoin having actually hit an all-time high $1,400 recently.

Traffic jams will unquestionably restrict deal volumes over the near-term, leaving the door open for more standard payment approaches to contend, but it is only going to refer time right before payment systems are updated and Bitcoin has the chance to become a main payment system.

In the end, the success and advancement of Bitcoin right across traditional economies and beyond will likely come down to the mindsets of Reserve banks.

The PBoC previously in the year had revealed that it would be making a higher effort to manage the Bitcoin market, consisting of developing a taskforce to examine and make sure Bitcoin exchanges had the proper anti-money laundering systems, alerting exchanges that they would be shut down if in infraction. The actions of the PBoC caused certain exchanges suspending activity, leading to Bitcoin losses at the time. Eventually the simple fact that the PBoC is seeking to tidy up and increase oversight is a long-lasting positive and suggests that making use of Bitcoin will rise in the years ahead, in spite of the fall over the near-term credited to the increased oversight.

The intents of Satoshi Nakamoto was eventually to knock reserve banks off their perch, the developer of Bitcoin openly going over a mistrust tos reserve banks. The development of Bitcoin has definitely opened the eyes of lots of, bringing into question the requirement for reserve banks should Bitcoin become the technique of choice, as there would be no requirement for the issuance and settlement.

Making use of Bitcoin might eliminate certain roles of main lenders, but in the end Bitcoin will never ever be accountable for and even be in a position to affect financial policies. Reserve banks will continue to eventually to hold the fate of Bitcoin in their hands, policy and approval at federal government level essential to its success and continued advancement cross border. In the meantime, reserve banks seem vigilantly checking out the innovation that Bitcoin has introduced, wanting to use the decentralized approach of record keeping, more typically called the blockchain or dispersed journal, the reward being to finish and log deals in a genuine economy better.

The BoE and the PBoC are definitely supporters of the decentralized approach that would enable the particular reserve banks to track their particular currency through the monetary system in real time. The BoE has approximated that using a digital currency on a dispersed journal could include as much as 3% to a nation's financial output through performance gains alone.

FOMC members and the FED Chair have also talked favorably on dispersed journals, with voting-member Brainard having actually spoken on the advantages of using such ingenious innovation just recently.

Surprisingly, the simple fact that Reserve banks are starting to embrace the innovation, which had been developed to dismiss them could eventually seal the position and power of reserve banks, though it would be challenging for them to then try to unwind the extremely exact same innovation in a quote to weaken Bitcoin down the roadway.

Bitcoin might have a combined following at present, but there are some nations that are eventually thought about the Bitcoin friendly, with the list very likely to continue growing as more federal governments acknowledge and legitimise making use of Bitcoin.

THE BITCOIN PROCEDURE: HOW IT WORKS

Bitcoin is a kind of digital money that permits online payments between the purchaser and the seller. It works as a digital journal that tape-records deals and balances of accounts.

Bitcoins are exchanged using the Bitcoin Procedure built over the concepts of cryptography. The procedure specifies the process that is followed by a Bitcoin deal from its creation, through recognition and last verification.

At the core of procedure is the Bitcoin deal system. Bitcoins are spent from electronic Bitcoin Wallets and are exchanged using Bitcoin deals. In order to comprehend the procedure, let us initially try to comprehend a deal, the info it consists of and how this info is processed.

Bitcoin Deals

A Bitcoin deal basically consists of the following info:

ID: Distinct deal ID which is the SHA256 double-hash of the deal information.

Input: The bitcoin addresses that recognize the sources of the bitcoins to be moved. These are normally a previous deal's output and are used to confirm the sender and check the readily available balance.

Amount: The number of bitcoins to be moved.

Output: The receiver's bitcoin address. In cases where there is remaining bitcoin change, the output needs to also consist of an entry for the sender's address to send it back, to be gathered as Deal Charge" or to be sent out to another receiver.

Outputs from one deal can be used as inputs for another deal. This produces a chain of ownership as the bitcoin value is moved from address to address.

Deal Recognition

All digital money deals also really need to be checked and confirmed for credibility, duplicity, and money accessibility. The recognition of the deals is not centralized and all taking part nodes are licensed for it.

A Bitcoin Wallet account that starts a payment deal is determined by a Bitcoin address and a set of public and personal secrets. To allow confirmation of the sender identity, deals are digitally signed using the sender's personal key and confirmed using his public key that is readily available to all the nodes.

The Bitcoin system orders the deals into lists called blocks. These are consequently connected to form a blockchain, a shared public journal of all verified deals. Deals not yet included in the blockchain are unofficial and reversible.

The miners validate and write these deals into the blockchain. To stop double-spending, a deal is not significant verified till it has gotten a particular number of verifications.

Each bitcoin mining node keeps an individual copy of the BlockChain which is upgraded whenever a brand-new deal shows up. This post clarified that GPU is also a really effective tool for the quick mining of bitcoins. Consequently, it also tries to verify the present and previous deals in the block by solving a mathematical puzzle called the Evidence of Work. The effective node that fixes the puzzle gets a Bitcoin benefit and its BlockChain authorized and accepted by all nodes.

The Bitcoin Procedure

In regards to the deal creation and recognition procedure, the Bitcoin Procedure can be mentioned as beneath:

A brand-new deal is relayed to all getting involved nodes in the network.

Each node gathers brand-new deals into a block.

Each node tries to confirm the brand-new deal and all previous ones by finding a resolution to the Evidence of Work for the block.

The node which finds the resolution transmits the fixed block to the network.

Nodes confirm the deals in the block and accept the block.

Nodes begin working on the next block. A hash of the last accepted block is created and used as a referral in the next block.

Summary

The Bitcoin procedure is based upon collaboratively preserving the Bitcoin journal. The digital money is moved through deals which are validated only after recognition of crucial requirements and joint agreement by taking part nodes through a mathematical puzzle based ballot procedure.

Chapter 17: Mining for Bitcoin

Bitcoin mining is the procedure by which deals are confirmed and contributed to the general public journal, referred to as the block chain, and also the ways through which brand-new bitcoin are released. Anybody with access to the web and appropriate hardware can take part in mining. The mining procedure includes putting together current deals into blocks and attempting to resolve a computationally hard puzzle. The individual who initially resolves the puzzle gets to put the next block on the block chain and declare the benefits. The benefits, which incentivize mining, are both the deal charges connected with the deals assembled in the block in addition to freshly released bitcoin.

The amount of brand-new bitcoin released with each mined block is called the block benefit. The block benefit is cut in half every 210,000 blocks, or approximately every 4 years. The block benefit began at 50 in 2009, is now 25 in 2014, and will continue to reduce. This decreasing block benefit will lead to an overall release of bitcoin that approaches 21 million.

How tough are the puzzles associated with mining? Well, that depends upon how much effort is being taken into mining right across the network. The problem of the mining can be changed, and is changed by the procedure every 2016 blocks, or approximately every 2 weeks. The trouble changes itself with the aim of keeping the rate of block discovery constant. Therefore if more computational power is employed in mining, then the trouble will change upwards to make mining harder. And if computational power is taken off of the network, the opposite happens. The problem changes downward to make mining simpler.

In the earliest days of Bitcoin, mining was finished with CPUs from typical home computer. Graphics cards, or graphics processing systems (GPUs), are more efficient at mining than CPUs and as Bitcoin acquired appeal, GPUs ended up being dominant. Ultimately, hardware referred to as an ASIC, which represents Application-Specific Integrated Circuit, was created particularly for mining bitcoin. The very first ones were released in 2013 and have been surpassed since, with more effective designs coming to market. Mining is competitive and today can only be done beneficially with the most recent ASICs. When using CPUs, GPUs, and even the older ASICs, the expense of energy usage is greater than the earnings produced.

MORE BITCOIN MINING APPROACHES

Bitcoin mining is the technique in which deals on the Bitcoin blockchain are verified and processed. If there were no Bitcoin miners, the Bitcoin cryptocurrency would stop to operate as no deals would be validated.

Those who perform the mining procedure are described as Bitcoin miners and they're rewarded for their help with a portion of the deal charge credited the Bitcoin user.

Mining Bitcoin can be a reliable way to make money and tons of people have now ended up being full-time Bitcoin miners. Here are the 3 primary methods to mine Bitcoin and begin making money.

Novice: Using a Bitcoin Mining App

The most convenient way to begin mining Bitcoin is to just download an app that does every little thing for you. Bitcoin Miner is a Windows 10 app that's totally free to download and use on Windows 10 PCs and tablets and also works on Windows Phones.

As Soon As the Bitcoin Miner app is downloaded, users just really need to enter their Bitcoin wallet's address in the Payment Address settings screen and after that push the popular Start button. That's all there is to it.

The more effective your gadget is, the more Bitcoin deals it will have the ability to procedure. This means that a Windows Phone might not make much Bitcoin but a Windows 10 computer system that can perform sturdy jobs like video modifying and playing significant computer game titles does have the possible to make a fair bit.

Newbie: Mine Bitcoin in the Cloud

A well-known way to participate the cryptocurrency mining trend is to pay somebody else to do it for you. Described as cloud mining, this procedure includes registering for an account on a third-party's site and paying them to mine Bitcoin and other cryptocurrencies for you.

Usually, the more cash you pay, the more cryptocurrency your account will have the ability to mine.

Cloud mining contracts generally last for a minimum of a year or so, though some can continue forever. Mined cryptocurrency is sent out to your designated wallet address regularly and this makes it a cool way to make recurring earnings on a weekly (or in some cases day-to-day) basis. The cryptocurrency that's mined usually covers the expense of the preliminary payment.

Genesis Mining is just one of the more credible cloud mining businesses around. Their creator and CEO has even given a TED Speak about its creation and the early days of Bitcoin mining. Genesis Mining offers Bitcoin mining contracts in addition to Litecoin, Ethereum, Monero, and a series of other cryptocurrencies.

Advanced: Structure a Bitcoin Mining Rig

Those aiming to actually purchase cryptocurrency mining will really need to purchase an application-specific integrated circuits (ASIC) hardware gadget, typically described as a mining rig. These are basically processors that are made exclusively for mining Bitcoin and other cryptocoins and are planned to run non-stop throughout the day, every day.

ASIC miners are typically rather pricey and cost some thousand dollars.

Running such a gadget also takes in a ton of electrical power so it can take a while, usually over a year of constant mining, to start making a revenue.

The most-popular brand name of ASIC miners is Bitmain with their Antminer miners. They typically launch more recent models of their miners that are more effective at mining Bitcoin and consuming energy and supply customers with detailed assistance and written set-up guides focused on both sophisticated miners and complete novices.

When using an ASIC mining gadget, you'll also really need to download innovative mining software application and join a mining pool. The software application will tell the ASIC what to mine, where to mine, and who to send out the mined Bitcoin to while the mining pool is a group of other miners that choose to help one another mine together and share the benefits between them.

The most frequently suggested mining pool and program is Slush Swimming pool and CGminer respectively nevertheless those using a Bitmain miner might choose to use their own program and mining pool because of their benefit and easy to use user interface.

Why You Must Mine Bitcoin

In addition to making money, mining a cryptocurrency can also be a way to support your favored coin. Miners are needed to process all deals on a crypto coin's blockchain so the more miners there are the faster and more steady the coin will be.

Why You Should Not Do Bitcoin Mining

Mining Bitcoin and other cryptocurrencies takes in a ton of cash, time, and resources. For many people it can be nearly as rewarding to just acquire some Bitcoin from a service like Coinbase or CoinJar and let it increase in value while being in a wallet not doing anything.

Trouble in Bitcoin Mining

The Computationally-Difficult Issue

Bitcoin mining a block is hard since the SHA-256 hash of a block's header need to be lower than or equivalent to the target in order for the block to be accepted by the network.

This issue can be streamlined for clarification functions: The hash of a block need to begin with a particular number of absolutely nos. The possibility of computing a hash that begins with lots of absolutely nos is really low; for that reason a lot of efforts need to be made. In order to create a brand-new hash each round, a nonce is incremented. See Evidence of work for more info.

The Bitcoin Network Trouble Metric

The Bitcoin mining network problem is the step of how hard it is to find a brand-new block compared to the most convenient it can ever be. It is recalculated every 2016 blocks to a worth such that the previous 2016 blocks would have been created in precisely 2 weeks had everybody been mining at this problem. This will yield, typically, one block every 10 minutes.

As more miners join, the rate of block creation will increase. As the rate of block generation goes up, the problem arises to compensate which will push the rate of block creation back down. Any blocks released by destructive miners that do not meet the needed problem target will just be turned down by everybody on the network and hence will be useless.

The Block Reward

When a block is found, the originator might award themselves a particular number of bitcoins, which is agreed-upon by everybody in the network. Presently this bounty is 25 bitcoins; this value will cut in half every 210,000 blocks.

Furthermore, the miner is rewarded the costs paid by users sending out deals. The cost is a reward for the miner to consist of the deal in their block. In the future, as the number of brand-new bitcoins miners are enabled to produce in each block diminishes, the charges will comprise a lot more crucial portion of mining earnings.

Chapter 18: What Is Ethereum?

Ethereum is more than a cryptocurrency. It's an open basis shared world calculating platform. Blockchain innovations are now simple to utilize without needing to transform the wheel all credit to Ethereum,

It is clear that Ethereum outgrew desire to use Bitcoin principles to worlds beyond cash. As a result, it offers open source platform to designers who try to write decentralized applications. These attract designers who look for a simple intro to Blockchain projects

A series of ingenious functions certain Ethereum. As a result of its prolonged capabilities, Ethereum features 2 kinds of accounts. EOA, or Externally Owned Accounts, offer bitcoin-like abilities like supplying a balance that is protected by personal secrets. Agreement Accounts offer the Turing Complete room for application development that makes the procedure so preferable.

These accounts are used as holding challenge make up Smart-contracts which supply Ethereum's ability for accommodating decentralized self-governing companies; a way of structuring companies without a susceptible center.

Most importantly, Ethereum profit from the awareness that agreement enables currency and currency enables agreement by supplying financial reward. As such, confirmations are paid for on a pay-per-use basis, a system that changes mining as we know it from Bitcoin.

THE DISCOVERY OF ETHEREUM

VitalikButerin, whose persistence to completely change the web, developed a platform on which designers could build any kind of decentralized application. With his in-depth grasp of Bitcoin, he suggested that it needed a scripting language for application development. When no one had an interest in his tip, he continued with his work on his effective brand-new job.

In 2013, he released a white paper defining this vibrant brand-new platform which he called Ethereum. For his amazing development, he was called as the 2014 Thiel Fellow and got a $100,000 award.

After this, vitalik quit the University of Waterloo to go after his Ethereum aspiration. With the assistance of other designers and co-founders, the task was rapidly moved into overdrive.

With a really effective crowd sale in July 2014, they raised more than $18 million by selling ether, the Ethereum tokens which were essentially the shares of the task.

A year later, their very first release called Frontier was launched on July 30, 2015. A brand-new platform was now readily available on which designers could develop their decentralized apps and clever agreements.

Ether is the 2nd biggest cryptocurrency on the planet and at one phase in 2017 it had a market capitalization of nearly $38 billion.

ETHEREUM MEANING

Ethereum is a decentralized software application platform that allowsSmartContracts and Dispersed Applications (ÐApps) to be created and run with no downtime, scams, control or disturbance from a 3rd party. Ethereum is not just a platform but also a shows language (Turing complete) working on a blockchain, assisting designers to build and release dispersed applications. The prospective applications of Ethereum are large range.

The applications on Ethereum are worked on its platform-specific cryptographic token, ether. Throughout 2014, Ethereum had launched a pre-sale for ether which had gotten a frustrating reaction. Ether is a lot like a car for moving on the Ethereum platform, and is looked for by mainly designers seeking to develop and run applications inside Ethereum. Ether is used broadly for 2 functions; it is traded as a digital currency exchange like other cryptocurrencies and is used inside Ethereum to run applications and even to generate income from work. The present market cap of ether (ETH) is now more than Ripple and Litecoin though it's far behind bitcoin (BTC).

According to Ethereum, it can be used to codify, decentralize, protect and trade practically anything.

How ether's market works

Unlike bitcoin, ether is not created to work as a worldwide digital currency. Instead, it is meant to pay for particular actions on the Ethereum network, with users getting it for using their computing power to confirm deals and for adding to its development

Nevertheless, ether's market is presently supported by tons of the exact same exchanges and facilities that has developed around the bitcoin network. For instance, users who have traditionally purchased bitcoin and other digital currencies on venture-backed exchange platforms just like Bitfinex and Kraken can today purchase ether on these sites.

But, ether's market did not develop in the exact same way as bitcoin's market.

In bitcoin, users were once able to process deals on the network using a personal computer, and after that ultimately, home mining devices. Bitcoin grew in value as the number of individuals in the network broadened. Ethereum probably developed under different situations.

In a quote to galvanize an international development community around its idea, Ethereum launched a pre-sale of ether tokens in 2014, raising more than $14m in what has been called a crowd financing effort, but bears similarity to a sort of casual going public (IPO).

In the bitcoin network, the supply rate is more constant. Due to hard-coded guidelines in the software application there will only ever be 21 million bitcoins (unless the guidelines are changed), and the rate at which brand-new tokens are introduced is 25 BTC approximately every 10 minutes today.Investors should keep in mind that such consistency is not ensured in the ether market.

The Ethereum Structure revealed at the time of launch that ether's guidelines would quickly change, and that beginning a long time in 2017, the network would follow the guidelines of Casper, an agreement algorithm still being developed.

Since mid-April, the overall number of ether deals stood at 3.3 million, leading to an ether supply of 79m ETH, Etherscan figures expose.

How does mining impact cost?

Among the largest elements on bitcoin's cost is the consistent intro of brand-new bitcoins through payments to the computer system operators that process deals (miners).

Mining impacts cost by increasing the supply, and through the choice of miners to hold or sell bitcoin. Ethereum's present variation, Homestead, leverages a proof-of-work based agreement algorithm, fulfilling computer systems that add to its security in the exact same way.

Under this system, miners produce a brand-new block every 15-17 seconds, leading to the creation of 5 ETH, according to figures offered by Ethereum.org. Miners that add to finding a resolution, but do not get their block included, can get 2 or 3 brand-new ethers, which is called an uncle/aunt benefit.

Once Ethereum begins using Casper, a proof-of-stake procedure, this rate is expected to change, as tons of prepare for Casper will supply a smaller sized mining aid. Under the brand-new procedure, nodes will not have the ability to verify deals and for that reason produce blocks unless they supply a down payment.

Should the procedure figure out that a node, or "bonded validator," has produced anything void, the node will lose both any deposit supplied and also the capability to take part in the agreement procedure? Presently, bonded validators deal with no charge if they produce blocks thought about void by the procedure.

By changing rewards, it is expected that Casper will be more effective, but the change could also mean that ether's value is adapted to the brand-new truths of the network's operation.

ETHEREUM CRITICISM

With 7 years of development (and couple of significant concerns), the bitcoin network is typically declared by fans as the most safe and secure blockchain. Even business companies have uttered a worth in its strong network results and varied mining network.

Ethereum has dealt with criticism for prospective security issues for some reasons, though the majority of center on the simple fact that the software application is in its early phases and has only been readily available for several years. The network has suffered less attacks than bitcoin, and as a result it has gone through less screening than its older digital currency.

The varying structures of ether and bitcoin's mining swimming pools are also worth keeping in mind. While bitcoin's mining community has in some cases drawn criticism for being controlled by a little number of gamers, this circumstances appears reproduced in Ethereum.

Farther, though the biggest bitcoin miner (F2Pool) represented 26% of the digital currency's hashrate circulation in this 24-hour block, the largest ether miner (dwarfpool) provided 41.8% of the currency's hashrate.

Moving forward, designers continue to work on more recent variations of Ethereum, but critics have anticipated that ether will deal with greater security issues than bitcoin. There is only one way to figure it out.

DISTINCTIONS IN BETWEEN ETHEREUM AND BITCOIN?

Ethereum has a somewhat different financial model than Bitcoin block benefits cut in half every 4 years whilst Ethereum launches the exact same amount of Ether each year advertisement infinitum.

Ethereum has a various technique for costing deals depending upon their computational intricacy, bandwidth usage and storage requirements. Bitcoin deals contend similarly with one another. This is called Gas in Ethereum and is restricted per block whilst in Bitcoin, it is restricted by the block size.

Ethereum has its own Turing complete inner code ... a Turing-complete code means that given enough calculating power and adequate time ... anything can be determined. With Bitcoin, there is not this form of versatility.

In Ethereum the block time is set to 14 to 15 seconds compared to Bitcoins 10 minutes. This enables faster deal times. Ethereum does this by utilizing the Ghost procedure.

Ethereum was crowd financed whilst Bitcoin was released and early miners own the majority of the coins that will ever be mined. With Ethereum 50% of the coins will be owned by miners in year 5.

Ethereum dissuades central pool mining through its Ghost procedure fulfilling stagnant blocks. There is no benefit to being in a swimming pool in regards to block proliferation.

Ethereum uses a memory tough hashing algorithm called Ethash that reduces against using ASICS and motivates decentralized mining by people using their GPU s.

Bitcoin sells cryptocurrency, while Ethereum offers some techniques of exchange consisting of cryptocurrency (Ethereum's is called Ether), wise contracts and the Ethereum Virtual Device (EVM).

They are based upon different security procedures: Ethereum uses an evidence of stake system as opposed the evidence of work system used by Bitcoin.

Bitcoin permits only public (permissionless or censor-proof) deals to occur; Ethereum enables both permissioned and permissionless deals.

For Bitcoin, the computer systems (called miners) running the platform and confirming the deals get benefits. Generally, the very first computer system that fixes each brand-new block gets bitcoins (or a portion of one) as a benefit. Ethereum doesn't provide block benefits and instead enables miners to take a deal charge.

SMART contracts ETHEREUM SIGNIFICANCE AND APPLICATIONS

Smart contracts are blockchain based contracts that are performed as quickly the hidden conditions are matched. Since there is no central authority, these contracts are devoid of scams, disturbance or speculation. These contracts can be used to help with the exchange of anything important like cash, shares, content, and so on.

Though using wise contracts sounds intriguing, there are serious ramifications associated with development. Once live the clever agreement will be carried out and there is no chance to stop it. For this reason, it crucial to carry out such contracts after comprehensive analysis.

Ethereum works as a platform to make it possible for the execution and development of such agreements. All blockchain applications built on Ethereum use some type of wise agreement for deal processing. In the lack of a blockchain platform like Ethereum, the whole blockchain needs to hardcoded. Now, designers can use the Ethereumblockchain for fast development and launch.

Applications of Ethereum:

Ethereum permits designers to develop decentralized applications that operate on a blockchain. A Dapp or decentralized app is a software application code that can run forever offered there suffices calculating power readily available. Since there is no central authority, Dapps cannot be managed or controlled. Bitcoins, for example, is also a decentralized application though it is not built using Ethereum.

It can also go a big step ahead and develop a completely self-governing decentralized company i.e. DAO. These companies are created based upon a collection of clever contracts that govern their performance. For this reason there is no requirement for a leader. In case of a DAO, the members own the ballot rights based upon their contributions. With Ethereum, it is possible to decentralize any central system just like banking, post, insurance coverage claims, and so on.

APPLICATIONS OF Smart Contracts

1. Insurance coverage

Due to an absence of automated administration, it can take months for an insurance coverage claim to be processed and paid. This is as bothersome for insurance provider as it is for their clients, causing admin expenses, excess, and ineffectiveness. Smart contracts can streamline and improve the procedure by immediately setting off a claim when certain events happen. For instance, if you resided in a part that was hit by a natural catastrophe and your home sustained damage, the clever agreement would acknowledge this and start the claim. Particular specifics (such as the degree of damage) could be made a record of on the blockchain to figure out the precise amount of payment. The exact same series of events would happen following a vehicle mishap, or if someone reported a guaranteed individual gadget as taken.

2. Supply chain management

Supply chain management includes the flow of products from basic material to complete item. Smart contracts can make a record of ownership rights as products move through the supply chain, verifying who is accountable for the item at any given time. This has ended up being far simpler using Web of Things sensing units, which track products from manufacturers to storage facilities, from storage facilities to producers, and from makers to providers.

The completed item can be validated at each phase of the shipment procedure till it reaches the consumer. If a product is postponed or lost, the wise agreement can be sought advice from to learn precisely where it needs to be. If any stakeholder stops working to meet the regards to the agreement, for example if a provider did not send out a delivery on time, it would be clear for every single party to see. Making supply chains more transparent by means of clever contracts is assisting to ravel the movement of items and bring back rely on trade.

3. Home loan

The home mortgage procedure is far from easy. The regards to a home mortgage arrangement, for instance, are based upon an evaluation of the mortgagee's earnings, outgoings, credit rating and other scenarios. The requirement to perform these checks, usually through 3rd parties, can make the procedure prolonged and complex for both the lending institution and the mortgagee. Eliminate the middle guys, though, and parties could deal straight with one another (along with access all the pertinent specifics in one area). As a basic rule, the easier something is, the more affordable it will be and through clever agreements, United States lending institutions alone could apparently save a minimum of $1.5 bn.

4. Employment agreement

The relationship between a worker and their company can be tempestuous, particularly if either party stops working to meet expectations. By participating in a clever agreement, a worker would know precisely what was expected of them, as would the company. Recording interactions in this way could help to enhance fairness in salaries or conditions, as any changes to contracts would be made a record of.

This openness could significantly enhance the relationship between companies and their staff members. Smart contracts could furthermore be used to assist in wage payments, according to the agreed amount and within a particular period. Smart contracts could also help to manage making use of short-lived labour, which includes a company, a firm and an employee.

The worker joins the firm and is then employed by a company. Sadly, an absence of openness has meant that firms can change the agreement's terms after workers have already begun the job. This could mean reducing or extending the agreement, changing wage rates or other worker's rights. It can be challenging for the authorities to find these changes, but not if a wise agreement system is used.

5. Securing copyrighted content

Each time that a piece of content is used for business functions, for instance a tune, the owner of the rights to that tune gets a royalty cost in theory. Obviously, there are several parties associated with creating a tune, and it can be tough to work out who owns these rights and who is for that reason entitled to payment, plus existing systems do not work well.

This has resulted in confusion over privilege, no doubt giving some contributors more than they are because of the hinderance of other ones while some get absolutely nothing at all. Smart contracts can make sure that royalties go to the designated receivers by tape-recording ownership rights in a decentralisedblockchain system. This could in theory be applied to any piece of content with a group of contributors.

Smart contracts have lots of advantages for a vast array of markets, lowering unneeded expenses and time expense while boosting openness. In theory, they are more effective and reliable than conventional agreement law, and are also believed to use better security as all actions are made a record of and confirmed. Nevertheless, like paper agreements, they could still experience scams. Code is not foolproof and can be postponed, obstructed and damaged. As organisations progress into digital settlements, an awareness of these dangers is essential.

What is Solidity?

Solidity is referred to as a contract-based, top-level programs language. This platform has comparable syntax to the scripting language of JavaScript. Solidity as a shows language is made to boost the Ethereum Virtual Device. Solidity is statically typed scripting language which does the procedure of validating and imposing the restraints at compile-time instead of run-time.

These typed shows languages will help and do the monitoring at run-time rather than Compile-time. This platform also supports inheritance in object-oriented shows; inheritance allows brand-new challenge handle the homes of existing things. A class that is used as the basis for inheritance is called a superclass or base class. A class that acquires from a superclass is called a subclass or obtained class. As you will see, it is possible to produce contracts for ballot, crowd financing, blind auctions, multi-signature wallets and more.

Ethereum Language

The source code in Ethereum language is written in Solidity variation 0.4.0 which doesn't break performance.

The very first line of code pragma Solidity agreement doesn't all of a sudden behave in a different way with a brand-new compiler variation. According to the docs, the keyword pragma is called that way since, in general, pragmas are guidelines for the compiler about how to deal with the source code. Pragma once is a preprocessor directive that tells the compiler to consist of the source code once in a single collection.

The line system saved information announces a state variable called kept information of type system. The functions set and can be used to customize or obtain the value of the variable. Actually believe it or not, this is an Ethereum agreement, though a rather easy offer.

The functions of the agreement enable you or anybody to save a single number that is available by anybody worldwide without a practical way to stop you from releasing this figure. Anybody could just call set again with a various value and overwrite your number, but the number will still be kept in the history of the blockchain. The line system kept information announces a state variable called kept information of type system.

The example above is the easiest form of an Ethereum agreement. Like learning mathematics, this agreement is comparable to including and deducting. Certainly, mathematics is more complex than just including and deducting, but at the basic level, all of the mathematics can be broken down into addition/subtraction operations.

HOW TO BUY ETHEREUM

In 2017, Ethereum has grown at an exceptionally quick speed. In simple fact, the third-largest cryptocurrency by market capitalization. It was at one point poised to take control of the top of the list, displacing Bitcoin to become the most popular cryptocurrency worldwide in a phenomenon called the "Flippening", till Ripple occurred.

Furthermore, Ethereum's coin, ether, has grown in value by lots of times since the start of the year, and some experts actually believe the cryptocurrency market still has brand-new heights to accomplish in the weeks and months to come. For all of these reasons, a lot more financiers are ending up being thinking about including Ethereum to their portfolios. Here is how to incorporateEthereum into your financial investments.

1. Develop an Account on an Exchange

Like other cryptocurrencies, Ethereum must be acquired and sold by means of an exchange online. There are certain these services that are readily available and are thought about highly trustworthy. Some of the most well-known consist of Coinbase, Kraken, Bitstamp, and Gemini. Right before you can begin trading Ethereum, you'll really need to choose an exchange and produce an account.

2. Validate the Account

Any credible exchange will need that you confirm your account in several methods. You'll likely really need to submit some files to confirm your identity and guarantee that your account passes regulative muster. Confirmation will generally take a day or more, depending upon how well-known and busy the exchange you have picked is.

3. Deposit Fiat Currency

You'll next really need to deposit fiat currency into your account, generally through bank or wire transfer. This might take another couple of days so as to guarantee that the cash clears.

4. Begin Trading

With a validated account and cash transferred into that account, you'll have the ability to start acquiring Ethereum and other cryptocurrencies by means of the exchange. Each exchange has a user interface that works rather in a different way, but be prepared to verify deals and after that permit processing time, which can also depend upon the overall number of deals asked for.

5. Withdraw ETH into a Wallet

Once you have bought ETH through the exchange, you can then withdraw that currency into a wallet that you manage. Exchanges can be hacked, indicating your tokens can be taken. In order to keep your tokens in a personal spot which you have access to by means of key, download and set up a wallet which has Ethereum abilities. Run and established the wallet, creating a brand-new account.

You can then input your account address into the exchange to move your ether to your wallet. Make certain not to use your wallet address, password, and personal key, otherwise you might have trouble accessing your ether in the future. Transfer it back to the exchange to sell or continue trading at a later time.

Tips When Purchasing Ether

Do you remember while the different exchanges usually have comparable Ether rates, you are basically only trading with other ones on the specific exchange being used. So the rates will differ somewhat from exchange to exchange.

All United States exchanges will need identity confirmation and all have differing cash transfer policies in spot to adhere to anti-money laundering laws.

Traders should also look for tax guidance on how to report brief and long term capital gains on cryptocurrency, and keep in-depth records of all trades.

Finally, person's thinking about purchasing Ether needs to understand that all cryptocurrencies are presently incredibly unpredictable with costs that can increase or down considerably at any time - while this may supply a chance to make some fast gains, there is also the threat of sustaining considerable losses.

There are 2 fundamental trading techniques, when it concerns trading Ether.

Purchase and hold

Active trading

Purchase and Hold

Since there is a ton of upside potential in cryptocurrencies, there are tons of sellers that are taking a buy and hold technique. So if that is your method, you would just purchase some Ether and shop it in a safe spot.

This is called putting it into freezer.

What is a safe spot?

Well, there are 2 alternatives, paper wallets or hardware wallets. I would not suggest saving Ether in mobile apps, computer system wallets, exchanges or online wallets for any length of time. Those alternatives are great for short-term deals, but are not safe for long-lasting storage.

ETHEREUM VIRTUAL MAKER

EVM (or Ethereum virtual device) is the Ethereum clever contracts byte-code execution environment. Every node in the network runs EVM. All the nodes carry out all the deals that indicate clever contracts using EVM, so every node does the exact same estimations and shops the exact same worths. Deals that only move ether also need some computation, that is, to discover whether the address has a balance or not and subtract the balance appropriately.

Every node executes the deals and shops the last state as a result of different reasons. For instance, if there is a clever agreement that saves the names and specifics of everybody participating in a celebration, whenever a beginner is added, a brand-new deal is transmitted to the network. For any node in the network to show specifics of everybody participating in the party, they just really need to check out the last state of the agreement.

Every deal needs some calculation and storage in the network. For that reason, there needs to be a deal expense, otherwise the entire network will be flooded with spam deals, and also without a deal expense, miners will have no reason ...

WHAT ARE DAPPS?

" Dapp" is a mix of the words, or portmanteau, "decentralized application." Dapps are programs, tools, or applications that operate on the decentralized Ethereumblockchain.

The majority of people recognize with the common central applications they can download and work on their phones or computer systems. Central applications put trust information, content, account info, crucial performance into one primary entity: normally servers, information banks, or standalone computer systems. The Ethereum network, though, is community-based, unchecked by any single authority. This means Dapps might not be served from one main server, but instead can are on the network.

Routine apps have all their information originating from their own business servers and have one single authority. They need a user login that gathers your individuality information (name, birthdate, address, and so on). On the other hand, Dapps can sweat off the blockchain to work and just need a personal address (a random string of characters that holds no individual info) for users to visit.

Dapps are important as they can be used to link purchasers and sellers in markets, for sharing or saving files, keeping a virtual currency, and executing clever contracts all in a system without complete ownership or censorship. Some existing Dapps consist of image upload and storage tools, advertisement servers, security tools, and crowdfunding platforms. Other frequently used Dapps are digital wallets that act as a tool for handling and using Ether.

DECENTRALIZED APPS BEING DEVELOPED ON ETHEREUM

Referred to as a decentralized application, or 'dapp' for brief, the principle has been among the more unique ideas to arise from the blockchain community. Equipped with self-executing clever agreements, advocates of the innovation have imagined methods to change every little thing that today needs a central management, from organisations and services to federal governments.

In some methods, bitcoin could be thought about the very first dapp, as it is completely open-source, benefits contributors, runs without a main authority and uses blockchain innovation to help facilitate its continued usage case as an online currency.

Next-generation innovators are now trying to use these exact same concepts to a range of online services they really believe could be constructed in the dapp format, equipped with a little effort, knowledge and the will to charge forward into the unidentified.

Although a brand-new field, dapps are growing in number and lots of now exist in different phases of efficiency, from idea to working model and practical platform.

Ethereum' sdecentralisedblockchain and its native digital currency Ether are showing maybe the most commonly used tools for dapp structure, as its network is particularly built for the purpose and the Ethereum Structure, its trade company managing development, runs routine 'hackathon' events to promote brand-new decentralized applications.

But what can you do with a dapp?

For this function, CoinDesk casts its eye over the existing offerings and chooses 7 of the more intriguing projects being developed using the Ethereumblockchain.

Enhancing the web

Taking image or video on phone

The Vevue job assures to "bring Google Street View to life", by making it possible for users to take 30-second video of dining establishments, hotels, spots, events and more to share with other around the globe.

All users really need is a mobile phone, and by addressing demands pinned in their area they can make bitcoin and even Vevue equity tokens in picked regions.

In addition, with the job's Google Chrome extension, 'Vevues' are readily available when web browsers use Google Maps to search regional organisations.

The "Make Videos, Earn Bitcoin" app is already readily available on the Google Play shop, however is not in its last state and doesn't presently reward users.

Structure virtual worlds

Etheria game

Etheria is a Minecraft-like virtual world in which gamers can own tiles, 'farm' them for blocks and build things.

According to the task site, the "whole state of the world is kept in and all player actions are made through the decentralized, trustless Ethereumblockchain".

Previously, it mentions, all virtual worlds have been managed by a single entity. All elements of Etheria, on the other hand, are "consented to" by the individuals of the Ethereum network without main authority.

This means Etheria cannot be censored or removed by the federal government, by its "owner-players" or perhaps by the designer, 'fivedogit'. In impact, it will exist as long as Ethereum does.

Handling identity

Identity, personal privacy

In the digital age, the increasing threat of monetary criminal offense occurring from scams and identity theft shows the significance of a reputable methods to protect the person's identity.

To that end, KYC-Chain goals to offer agreement on the identity of people at the "greatest level of trust".

The service, which is presently under building and construction, uses existing know-your-customer (KYC) policies, and prepares to bring "ease and simpleness" to the procedure of recognition for companies wanting to onboard brand-new consumers.

The platform's "identity wallets" will enable users to share only the info essential, and absolutely nothing more.

KYC-Chain utilizes Ethereum and will work mainly through making use of "relied on gatekeepers", who can be any individual or legal entity allowed by law to confirm KYC files for instance, notary publics, people of diplomatic status, legal representatives, federal governments, and so on.

Assisting developing organisations

Development cash

4G Capital supplies immediate access to credit for small company development in Africa, and has developed a principle dapp for making use of wise agreements.

Donors would have the ability to use the dapp to money small companies in Kenya using digital currency. The cash provided would be transformed and paid out to the firms using 4G Capital's transactional system.

Its vision is to empower people, services and markets by providing monetary addition and supporting change right across Africa from the grass roots level.

In addition to supplying 100% unsecured financial obligation financing to self-employed casual market sellers, the job supplies micro-consulting and company training to increase client ability levels and company knowledge.

WeiFund uses Web 3.0-enabled innovation to supply a crowdfunding resolution on the Ethereum community.

The task says that since it will be among tons of crowdfunding platforms on Web 3.0, it aims to promote these platforms by supplying "first-rate open-source modular and extensible" crowdfunding energies that everybody can access. All important elements of the platform are entirely decentralized.

To use WeiFund, users will initially open WeiFund in a Web 3.0 made it possible for internet browser just like Ethereum's Mist. From there they can then begin, add to, search and manage crowdfunding projects.

WeiFund's user interface and user experience will be really comparable to that of standard crowdfunding platforms just like Kickstarter or GoFundMe, though, all funds raised on WeiFund will be represented in the Ether digital currency.

Unlike standard crowdfunding services like Kickstarter, however, WeiFund uses wise agreements, which means contributions can actually be developed into complicated contracts. This gives project operators a "wider variety of possibilities "when raising funds, the job says.

Chapter 22: The Thing about Augur

Augur is a decentralized forecast market which can anticipate the result of an occasion based upon the 'knowledge of the crowd' concept. With this technique, info gathered from the crowd is balanced into the most practical possibility and for that reason the most likely result. Right forecasts are rewarded by the network, while inaccurate reporting is punished - this incentivizes genuine reporting.

The Augur aims to change forecast markets, and, in doing so, changing the way people get and validate 'truth'. The main point is to make more precise forecasts by big groups of people, instead of a little group of professionals.

Augur is also the very first significant decentralized application (Dapp) developed using Ethereum, and represents a major evidence of principle for this underlying innovation. Decentralization makes sure that Augur cannot be censored by federal governments that consider forecast markets as betting, whilst making sure the sustainability of the application. This decentralized nature makes sure sincerity in reporting the result of events, using crowd knowledge to counteract individual scams.

Augur's crowdsale raised more than 2,000 BTC and 100,000 Ether on its very first day. It ran all the way from 17 August 2015 till 5 September 2015. The platform is presently in beta stage.

Augur coin

Credibility

The foundation of Augur is tradable tokens called Credibility (REPRESENTATIVE). The overall amount of Credibility is repaired at 11 million coins when it was launched in August 2015. The tokens give the right for people to report or weigh in on the result of events. It can be made by people who supply genuine reports.

Furthermore, people who submit right forecasts are also rewarded a part of the earnings whereas people who report against the agreement (untruthfully) will lose their REPRESENTATIVE tokens and make absolutely nothing. Additionally, the more REPRESENTATIVE a user has, the more value or trust is appointed to that person's input.

To put it simply, Track record tokens are gotten and lost depending upon the dependability of users votes with the agreement. The Augur Group released an infographic to clarify how the Credibility tokens work.

What Forecasts are used for

People can establish events in any subject and purchase shares for the possible results of those events. Ether and bitcoins are accepted in the platform. The algorithm will then deal with the crowdsourced info and offers leading forecasts based upon agreement. Once the event is concluded, the funds related to shares of the right result are dispersed to 'winners'.

Augur can be used beyond simple wagering platform. Joey Krug, co-founder and lead designer of Augur said that the platform 'could be used by farmers in Argentina to hedge against weather cycles or by Chinese dealers who are not able to access the United States stock exchange', and even suggests that 'forecast markets could be used by physicians to more precisely detect clients.'

Forecast markets are not brand-new principles, but it's highly decentralized nature means that Augur is rather untouched by restrictions set by guidelines.

Beginning With Augur

Augur is a decentralized open source forecast market, in Augur you will have the ability to make a forecast on anything and users will have the ability to purchase or sell shares in that forecast based upon whether they believe it will happen or not, this could be anything from the weather, to the winner of an election.

It is successfully wagering nevertheless the cost of each agreement will include of to $1 so if the chance of a result going on was even cash the agreement would cost 50 cents each and you could purchase or sell as a lot of as you wanted. The cost of an agreement will also immediately change based upon the number of contracts being purchased or sold.

Users will also have the ability to report on results this will make them track record and depending on how much credibility a person has will depend upon how precise their result reports are. Augur is built on the Ethereumblockchain as it will operate on wise agreements, there is also talk that it will run together with the Bitcoinblockchain so that both Ether and Bitcoin are tradeable within Augur.

Chapter 23: Track Record

Track record is the token behind Augur and can be considered ball game of a private participant within Augur. Track record is not a financial investment, but rather a tool required to make Augur work. The huge bulks of Augur individuals will never ever hold, see, or really need to use Credibility. Nevertheless, it's exceptionally crucial to comprehend how Track record operates in order to completely comprehend the Augur platform.

Credibility tokens are restricted to a repaired supply of 11,000,000, of which 80% was sold in our public token sale in 2015 for a cumulative ~$ 5,300,000. Those who hold Credibility are expected to report precisely on the result of arbitrarily picked events within Augur every couple of weeks.

If holders flop to report properly on the result of an occasion, or effort to be unethical the Augur system rearranges the bad press reporters Track record to those who have reported precisely throughout the exact same reporting cycle.

It's essential to keep in mind that you do not really need Credibility to use Augur. Credibility is only used by press reporters to report on the results of events. Routine individuals making bets on the platform will use Ether, or any other Ethereum sub currency. We intend to see the usage of stable-coins in the future for settlement of markets.

METRICS THAT SHOW ETHEREUM COULD OVERTAKE BITCOIN

Ethereum has 2 essential benefits over Bitcoin: one technological and one organizational. Whereas Bitcoin is a cryptocurrency only, Ethereum is a general-purpose platform for running blockchain-based apps, like a decentralized variation of iOS or Android. Ethereum consists of a cryptocurrency, Ether, plus anything else that software application designers want to produce for the platform. The series of possible usage cases is possibly unrestricted. This is why there are supposedly 30 times as a lot of designers working on software application associated to Ethereum than to any other blockchain innovation, consisting of Bitcoin.

Bitcoin struggles with an absence of strong management. Its pseudonymous developer Satoshi Nakamoto hasn't been spoken with in years. In the last 6th months, Bitcoin has divided into 2: Bitcoin and Bitcoin Money. On the other hand, Ethereum's developer VitalikButerin leads Ethereum development at the Ethereum Structure. Advancement appears to be working out. On December 31, Ethereum launched a test network for alpha screening of Casper, its execution of evidence of stake, a less computationally extensive way to verify deals

These 2 basic benefits lead me to really believe that at some time Ethereum will surpass Bitcoin in appeal and market price?? already, the overall flow of Ether is definitely worth $121 billion to Bitcoin's $259 billion. In simple fact, there are 4 metrics that show Ethereum has already exceeded Bitcoin in network efficiency and show arising appeal relative to Bitcoin.

1. Daily deals.

The Ethereum network processes 1.2 million deal daily. That's over 3 times more than the Bitcoin network, which only processes 354,000 deals daily.

2. Deal charges

To get a Bitcoin deal validated within 24 hr, it presently costs $7.19. To get a deal validated within 20 minutes, it costs $25.57. By contrast, to get an Ethereum deal verified in 30 seconds, it costs $1.59. Remember Ethereum is processing over 3 times as a lot of deals every day.

There seems abnormally high activity on the Ethereum network recently causing higher costs. Whenever I have checked out the last couple of weeks, the costs for Ethereum have been under 10 cents to get a deal verified in under a minute.

3. Active addresses

Given that December 31, the number of active Ethereum addresses has gone beyond the number of active Bitcoin addresses on 3 celebrations. Active addresses do not flawlessly represent number of active users, specifically since Ethereum addresses can be designated to software application like clever agreements. Nevertheless, higher activity on the network suggests that more people are getting more use out of it.

4. Nodes

Ethereum has 31,800 nodes to Bitcoin's 11,700. By number of nodes, the Ethereum network is already much bigger than the Bitcoin network.

Hashing functions are a vital part of cyber security and some cryptocurrency procedures like Bitcoin.

What is hashing?

Hashing is an approach of cryptography that transforms any form of information into a distinct string of text. Any piece of information can be hashed, no matter its size or type. In conventional hashing, no matter the information's size, type, or length, the hash that any information produces is always the exact same length. A hash is developed to function as a one-way function? You can put information into a hashing algorithm and get a distinct string, but if you come across a brand-new hash, you cannot figure out the input information it represents. A distinct piece of information will always produce the exact same hash.

How does it work?

Hashing is a mathematical operation that is simple to perform, but incredibly tough to reverse. (The distinction between hashing and file encryption is that file encryption can be reversed, or decrypted, using a particular key.) The most extensively used hashing functions are MD5, SHA1 and SHA-256. Some hashing procedures are considerably tougher to break than other ones. For instance, SHA1 is much easier to break than crypt.

Some examples of information go through SHA1 hashes. The SHA1 hashes will always be the exact same for this information.

Who uses hashing?

The typical user encounters hashing daily in the context of passwords. For instance, when you produce an e-mail address and password, your e-mail supplier likely doesn't save your password. Rather, the supplier runs the password through a hashing algorithm and saves the hash of your password. Each time you try to check in to your e-mail, the e-mail supplier hashes the password you get in and compares this hash to the hash it has conserved. Only when the 2 hashes match are you licensed to access your e-mail.

Hashing in Cryptocurrencies

In the Bitcoinblockchain, mining is basically carried out by running a series of SHA-256 hashing functions. In cryptocurrencyblockchains today, hashing is used to write brand-new deals, timestamp them, and eventually to include a recommendation to them in the previous block. When a block of deals is contributed to the blockchain, and agreement is reached amongst operators of different nodes (confirming that all of them have the right and real variation of the whole journal), it is almost unrealistic to reverse a deal because of the massive computing power that would be needed by anybody trying to damage the blockchain, and the one-way nature of the hashing. Hashing is for that reason essential to preserve the cryptographic stability of the blockchain.

Hashing and Cyber security

When a company finds that a platform's passwords have been jeopardized, it normally means that hackers have gotten the hashes that represent the passwords. Hackers then run the hashes of typical words and combos of typical words and numbers to figure out some of the passwords that users have conserved.

The cybersecurity market now uses a system called salting. Salting consists of including random information to a password right before hashing it, and after that keeping that salt value with the hash. This procedure makes it harder for hackers to use pre-computation methods and fracture passwords of hashed information that they have gotten.

Cryptographic hashing has long contributed in cybersecurity, and is now poised to power the coming wave of blockchain applications.

Chapter 25: More Ethereum Specifics

Gas keeps Ethereum Blockchain alive, thanks to it we can move Ether and other Ethereum tokens like: GameCredits (GAME), OmiseGo (OMG) or Golem (GNT), it also permits to clever contracts to do their job. In this blogpost I m going to clarify: what is Gas? how is it used? and why is it so essential for the future of Ethereum?

Fuel of the Blockchain.

Ethereumblockchain is run by nodes that keep the blockchain state but also determine brand-new blocks. New blocks are needed to change Blockchain's mention e.g. relocation Ethereum from one account to another. Estimation of the brand-new block is made by miners; to cover their effort deal sender should pay a cost. Deal cost depends upon intricacy of deal sender wants to make, if it's a routine send out.

Ether deal or more complicated one like produce clever agreement (wise agreement a unique sort of the blockchain account, that cannot only keep Ether but also computer system program with its state). Sending out Ether from one account to the other expenses 21,000 Gas. On the other hand creating wise agreement which is accountable for dealing with OmiseGo Token costed 1,197,977 Gas. So the more intricate deal, the more Gas we really need to pay for its execution on Blockchain. Main intricacy elements are:

Operations carried out by the wise agreement's code e.g. arithmetical operations.

Information that is kept on blockchain e.g. saving info in the clever agreement or upgrading a quantity of Ether on the account.

How much does Gas cost?

We know more or less what Gas is, but how much does it cost? The answer is as always it depends. Each deal sender (e.g. person who is sending out Ether) is specifying cost of Gas for created deal (e.g. 1 Gas = 0.000000001 ETH). If the cost is high enough, deal will be performed quicker, since miners will perform deals with the greatest gas cost first. If cost will be too low, we might wind up waiting long for execution of our deal. Tons of tools specifically wallets set deal cost by themselves not to hustle user and supply smoother experience, but it doesn't mean there is no cost.

How to set the Gas cost right? Lots of tools will give us default value that is enough e.g. Metamask but often we should change it (e.g. we really want this deal to be performed ASAP). There are data typically Gas cost and deal time readily available e.g. on GasStation or Etherscan that might help us setting the right cost.

Gas is not another currency; Gas is a measurement system of intricacy of the deal (the more complicated deal, the more Gas it will take in). The cost of Gas is specified by the sender but its miners choice in which order they will carry out deals. If you do not want to discover more about deal processing and computing Gas expense, skip that part and go to the next area.

There is a bit more of terms worth describing here. Let's try to evaluate 2 different deals in regards to Gas:

What Gas can tell us?

Gas may not only be the fuel of the Blockchain, it might also be a crucial source of info. Since Ethereum was created not only as crypto-currency but also to host dispersed applications (such us tokens), Gas has substantial influence on Ethereum's economy. Presently there are 10s and even numerous ERC20 certified (and non-ERC) tokens that work on EthereumBlockchain. Every deal of those tokens needs Gas; it's just a deal that calls a wise agreement's function after all.

The amount of all token deals is substantial and every one needs Gas, which is paid in Ethereum. To put it simply every token deal increasesEthereum need. On the other hand, every token transfer will increase miners benefit. In the near future proof-of-stake will change proof-of-work, this will result in the substantial decrease of the block benefit and Gas will become the primary miners earnings. So next time you will find out about ICO of the brand-new Ethereum token think: higher Ethereum need and more work (and Gas spend) for miners.

We might evaluate deals Gas use a lot more. The structure of Gas use and its difference in time will tell us how EthereumBlockchain is used and identify the innovation state. We may filter deal with ERC20 tokens and other dispersed applications (Dapplications or Dapps) and see: how much are they used? how much Gas/Ether is spent on interaction by their users? That might help us to find answers for the questions relating to future of Ethereum and design better Dapps.

Other essential aspect that we might evaluate is the Gas cost. Conduct of users that are sending out deals may be an intriguing location of research. It might also be an important to form Ethereum's Gas cost policies. Since the less expensive Gas is the less expensive expense of running Dapps. If Dapps will become more well-known, then higher deal volume will compensate lower Gas costs to the miners. On the other hand the more well-known EthereumBlockchain is, the higher deal throughput is expected. It might result in Blockchain's efficiency issues. Presently primary effort of Ethereum development is concentrated on efficiency, scalability and personal privacy. Solutions just like Casper or Plasma are just around the corner.

Cryptocurrency lovers venturing into the world of Ethereum for the first time will need to find out a thing or more in the beginning. Although the knowing curve is easy by any ways, there are some things people really need to consider. Among the most complicated elements is how the network uses gas to perform deals and contracts on the Ethereum network.

THE REQUIREMENT OF ETHEREUM's GAS.

Any cryptocurrency network uses some form of cost to perform deals or actions on the network. In the Bitcoin world, this is a percentage of BTC which is paid to the miners for consisting of the transfer in the next network block. On the Ethereum network, this charge is referred to as gas, which suggests an inner rates for each deal or agreement on the blockchain. This gas amount is really little, however, but it needs to be included in every action regardless.

Gas was introduced as part of the Ethereum environment so it could scale as needed. To be more particular, miners can increase or reduce the gas amount based upon how thing are searching the general network. More particularly, it is developed in such a way a greater ETH cost would not need all gas rates to be changed. Contrary to the Bitcoin environment where costs increase throughout blockage durations, miners can choose what to do on the Ethereum network.

One could argue there is a connection between Ethereum's gas cost and the way we gauge using electrical energy in Kilowatts. Nevertheless, the Ethereum network transcends in this regard, since the person creating the deal or agreement action sets the cost of gas. Miners are then completely free to accept or decline this proposition as they please. Additionally, the gas cost is rather vibrant, as can be seen on the Etherscan site.

Do not be misinterpreted in thinking Ethereum's network doesn't have a block size limitations, however. The gas cost is created to guarantee deals will be included in the next network block, comparable to how Bitcoin runs. Bitcoin miners focus on deals with the greatest charges out of individual gain. Ethereum miners can do the exact same, as it is their own choice to consist of lower-gas deals or not. A beneficial gas cost will get your network actions verified that much quicker, as is to be expected.

Gas is created to handle Ethereum's Turing Complete nature and the Ethereum Virtual Device Code. The tiniest denomination of gas should in theory enable anybody to carry out a line of code. Accounts that do not consist of sufficient gas to perform the deal will not have the ability to perform said action. By utilizing this technique, the Ethereum designers intend to nullify denial-of-service attacks and motivate effectiveness in the procedure code. Making an aggressor pay very much for the resources turned against the Ethereum network should stop most attacks.

As is to be expected, more intricate operations of the Ethereum network will need a greater gas cost. Forming agreements, for instance, is even more complex than just sending out funds straight to a various account. More intricate contracts need more computing power, which will also lead to a greater gas cost most times. It is a fascinating take on things, that much is certain.

Ethereum "Gas" - How it Functions

Purpose

Comprehending how gas works is important for Ethereum users thinking about taking part in ICOs, using wise agreements, and even making easy transfers between wallets. In this post, I wish to clarify what gas is and how it works. Skip to the end for a basic summary of things. To begin, we really need to comprehend some fundamentals about the Ethereum Virtual Device.

Ethereum Virtual Device and Gas

The Ethereum Virtual Device (EVM) is a huge part of the Ethereum environment, but I'll be greatly glossing over this so we can concentrate on how it associates with gas. Simply put, the EVM is an environment where approximate code of wise contracts and other operations can be carried out. Every node in the Ethereum network executes operations within the EVM to guarantee redundantly right execution and depends on agreement to settle on the answer.

All deals, from basic transfers to ICO wise agreements, need some amount of operations to perform. Each of these operations has an involved expense in gas. Therefore, easy deals like transfers will need less gas to perform than more extreme wise agreements.

For instance, an easy operation like if(var > 1) might cost 1 gas, but a more intricate operation to save a variable could cost 100 gas. The cumulative amount of all the operations is the overall gas expense for the deal.

Gas Limitation

When on a website like MyEtherWallet, you're visiting a field called Gas Limitation. This corresponds the OPTIMUM amount of gas you want to invest in the deal.

Essential to keep in mind:

Various kinds of deals will need different quantities of gas to finish

Supplying insufficient gas will lead to a stopped working deal, the charges are kept by the miner

Additional, unspent gas is reimbursed instantly

What happens if I define insufficient gas?

Your deal will begin to be carried out, but will ultimately run out of gas and be stopped. When this happens, you will not return ether invest in the gas used, but since the deal did not complete, the blockchain doesn't show a transfer, so the primary funds basically never ever left the wallet.

Gas Cost

Gas cost is the amount of ether you want to invest in every system of gas. Yes, you identify the cost of gas AND optimum amount of gas you want to invest in carrying out a deal on the Ethereum network. Although gas limitation is just an easy amount, gas cost is gauged in ether (particularly some amount of wei, normally gwei). The value of gas is driven by the market and the nodes that focus on higher gas costs when mining deals. The present gas cost can be seen on Etherscan or EthGasStation.

Summary

Deals on the Ethereum network need costs in the form of gas. The amount of gas depends upon the amount of calculation needed to finish the deal.

Gas Limitation is the optimum amount of gas allocated to the deal, 21000 sufficing for basic transfers and much higher quantities for transfers to wise contracts like those in ICOs.

Inadequate gas in the Gas Limitation will lead to a stopped working deal, the charge paid will be lost, but the ether moved never ever leaves the wallet since the blockchain was never ever upgraded.

Gas Cost is the cost of each gas system gauged in a fractional amount of ether, usually gwei. Gas cost differs, but 20-30 gwei is typical since writing this.

Current Gas Cost can be checked online (Etherscan or EthGasStation), and the Gas Limitation for things aside from easy transfers can only be understood by taking a look at the clever agreement code or by taking a look at what the company behind the ICO/ wise agreement says is proper for their clever agreement.

Chapter 26: VPNs for Greater Privacy

2017 has been a great year for cryptocurrency. Along with the incredible market gains that cryptocurrencies such has Bitcoin have experienced, cryptocurrency has shown vital in having the ability to safeguard user privacy and security. In a world in which our online personal privacy is relatively being deteriorated by central entities, the decentralized nature of cryptocurrency guarantees to give control back to the user.

You can truly really appreciate the requirement for greater user privacy when you recognize what centralized entities just like Facebook and Youtube are finishing with our information. When you use Facebook, you are talking about posts, liking posts, and usually giving info away on who you are. Facebook will save this information on you, and after that sell it to 3rd parties like marketers. These 3rd parties will then use this information to customize their advertisements that line up with your interests. For lots of, this is an unpleasant idea, as Facebook and these third-party marketers are basically making use of and benefiting from your information. Being a confidential user avoids this, by making sure that your info is encrypted and protected.

Cryptocurrency & VPNs

Bitcoin was the very first cryptocurrency that revealed us how cryptography and blockchain innovation could be used to reinforce user privacy. If you want to negotiate using Bitcoin, then you can do so through a Bitcoin address, which is not connected to any of your individual info. Nevertheless, it has quickly ended up being clear that Bitcoin is more pseudonymous than it is really confidential. This has added to the arise of cryptocurrencies like Monero and Zcash, that use much greater user privacy than Bitcoin. By utilizing cryptocurrencies just like Monero and Zcash, users have a lot more security and personal privacy defense when negotiating online.

Integrating cryptocurrency with a VPN (Virtual Personal Network) more boosts a user's privacy when using the web. A VPN works by masking your IP (Web Procedure) address so that your online activities are essentially unrealistic to trace. The significant advantage of using a VPN is that it is protecting your web connection, thus ensuring that all of your information is encrypted and protected from outdoors parties. In the exact same way that cryptocurrency offers personal privacy defense when negotiating and making online payments, a VPN offers defense for your web access. Utilizing a mix of both an anonymizedcryptocurrency and a VPN makes sure optimum user privacy when it concerns your online activities.

EVERYTHING YOU REQUIRED TO LEARN ABOUT Making Use Of LITECOINS

Litecoins are a kind of cryptocurrency that has grown in appeal in reaction to the need for alternative currency alternatives from customers all over the world. This currency works similar to basic world currencies. Traders and financiers have realized the great prospective this currency needs to provide, and it is greatly traded by starting and skilled financiers alike. The best way to get the most out of Litecoin trades is to use the services of a Litecoin broker. There are many Litecoin brokers readily available that have outstanding track records for supplying their customers with exceptional service. These brokers will have the ability to help sellers make noise choices about their financial investments.

When you employ a very good Litecoin broker, they will have many tools and resources readily available to make sure that your trades go efficiently. Maybe the most secondhand tool by these brokers is the Litecoin news widget. This widget can be completely personalized to meet your particular requirements. It will give consistent updates on cryptocurrency news and other pertinent info, so that you will be privy to the most recent news developments as they are released on the wires. The following will give insight on what precisely this cryptocurrency is and how it can be used and gotten in addition to trading for it.

What are Litecoins?

Litecoins are a type of virtual currency that can be acquired and used to purchase and sell different product and services just like fashion jewelry, clothes, food, and electronic devices. Since this currency is only used online, its value is determined by need on currency trading sites. This cryptocurrency can be traded, or it can be mined. When mining for the currency, the procedure can be a challenging job. Computer systems fixed mathematical formulas, and they are rewarded as a result. Almost any great computer system can mine for the currency, but statistically the chances of success are low and it can take days just to make a number of coins.

The primary distinction is that Litecoins can be acquired much faster than Bitcoins, and their limitation is set to 84 million, whereas Bitcoin's limitation is only 21 million in contrast. Bitcoins are accepted at more online shops, but Litecoins are being rising up in appeal each and every single day. The currency is decentralized, so this is a great benefit to dealers. The expense is anticipated to be lower than Bitcoin expenses, as the cryptocurrency ends up being more extensively understood.

Litecoin:

Launched in 2011, Litecoin is usually described as 'silver to Bitcoin's gold.' Charlie Lee - MIT graduate and previous engineer at Google - is the creator of Litecoin.

Comparable to Bitcoin, Litecoin is a decentralized, open source payment network which works without a main authority.

Litecoin resembles Bitcoin in a lot of methods and typically leads people to believe: "Why not go with Bitcoin? Both are comparable!" Here's a catch: the block generation of Litecoin is much faster than that of Bitcoin! and this is the primary reason merchants worldwide are ending up being more available to accepting Litecoin.

Litecoin is a decentralized online currency. It can be used to acquire web services, like site development or items, like jewellery or other associated devices. The great feature of Litecoin is that it supplies merchants with a safe and simple way to accept cash, as there are no charges when sending out or getting funds. You will also find that all payments are made a record of by means of an online system, otherwise referred to as the blockchain. This makes it possible for the payment receiver to instantly confirm the payment and the user, without needing to research all of it by hand.

Litecoin Worldwide

Litecoins can be used around the world, by anybody. The charges experienced by Litecoin users are substantially lower when compared to that of charge card businesses and bank transfers. For instance, a consumer in France can get a payment from somebody in New york city within seconds, with both parties acquiring clear evidence that the deal has gone through while also having it saved on the blockchain system. Litecoin uses software application which permits you to send out payments, just like sending out an e-mail. It is well worth keeping in mind that there will only ever be 84 million litecoins, so you do not really need to worry about inflation impacting the total value of your currency. Lots of people make exchanges using litecoins, with countless trades going on every day. These exchanges are typically used to trade Euros, dollars and more into litecoins, so the possibilities actually are limitless. This also allows users to safeguard their monetary investments by trading their physical currency into litecoins, so exchanges can happen without concern of the brand-new currency diminishing in value.

Whatever you really need, litecoins can be a great way to make online purchases, not to point out that they can also help you secure your own financial resources by safeguarding you from inflation and other external impacts that may impact the value.

Litecoin

Litecoin was Bitcoin's 2nd fiddle for rather a long time but things began changing early in the year of 2017. First, Litecoin was adopted by Coinbase together with Ethereum and Bitcoin. Next, Litecoin repaired the Bitcoin problem by adopting the innovation of Segregated Witness. This gave it the capability to lower deal charges and do more. The choosing aspect, though, was when Charlie Lee chose to put his sole concentrate on Litecoin and even left Coinbase, where're he was the Engineering Director, just for Litecoin. Due to this, the cost of Litecoin rose up in the last number of months with its greatest element being the simple fact that it could be a real option to Bitcoin.

A number of things to keep in mind:

When you established your wallet, if you click around a bit, you will see an alternative to pay a cost to speed deals. This cash appears to a bitcoin miner as he/she/they procedure bitcoin info. The miners doing the work of creating blocks of info keeps the system as much as date and protect. The charge is a reward to the miner to be sure to include your info in the next info block and for that reason "confirm" it. In the short-term, miners are making the majority of their cash by mining brand-new coins (check the area on What Are Bitcoins for additional information about this). In the long term, as it gets tougher to find brand-new coins, and as the economy increases, the costs will be a reward for miners to keep creating more blocks and keep the economy going. Your wallet ought to be set to pay 0 charges as a default, but if you really want, you can include a cost to prioritize your deals. You are under no responsibility to pay a charge, and tons of companies that process lots of little deals (like the ones that pan for gold defined above) produce sufficient costs to keep the miners happy.

In clicking around your wallet, on the deals page or connected to particular deals, you will see a note about verifications. When you make a deal, that info is sent into the network and the network will return a verification that there is no double entry for that bitcoin. It is wise to wait till you get some verifications right before leaving somebody who has paid you. It is actually not extremely simple to rip-off somebody hand-to-hand like this, and it is not really economical for the criminal, but it can be done.

Where can you purchase bitcoin like this?

You might have a bitcoin Meetup in your location.

You can have a look at localbitcoins.com to find people near you who have an interest in purchasing or selling.

See if you have any good friends who wish to try bitcoins out. Actually, the more people who begin using bitcoin, the bigger and more effective it will be come. So please tell 2 good friends!

Some people ask if it is possible to purchase physical bitcoins. The answer to this is both a yes and a no. Bitcoin, by its very nature, is a digital currency and has no physical form. Nevertheless, there are a number of ways in which you can virtually hold a bitcoin in your hands:

Cascascius Coins: These are the creation of Mike Caldwell. He mints physical coins and after that embeds the personal secrets for the bitcoins inside them. You can get the personal key by peeling a hologram from the coin which will then plainly show that the coin has been damaged. Mike has headed out of his way to make sure that he can be relied on. These are a very good financial investment method as in the years to come it might be that these coins are big collector's products.

Paper Wallets: A paper wallet just means that instead of keeping the info for your bitcoin kept in a digital wallet, you print the essential info off in addition to a personal key and keep it safe in a safe, in a drawer, or in your bed mattress (if you like). This is highly advised and cost reliable system for keeping your bitcoin safe. Bear in mind, however, that somebody could take them or if your home burns, they will choose the home and there will be no other way to get them back. Actually, no different than money. Also, similar to Casascius Coins, they will not truly benefit investing till you put them back into the computer system.

There is software application to make printing your paper wallets much easier. bitcoinpaperwallet.com is just one of the best and consists of a pretty good tutorial about how to use them.

The bitcoins are not actually in the wallet, they are still on the internet. In simple fact, the beyond the wallet will have a QR code that will enable you deliver coins to the wallet at any time you like.

The sealed part of the wallet will have the personal key without which you cannot access the coins. For that reason, only put as tons of coins on the wallet as you want to be unattainable. You will not have the ability to whip this thing out and take out several coins to purchase a cup of coffee. Rather, come up with it as a piggy bank. To get the cash, you need to smash it. It is possible to take out tinier quantities, but at this moment the security of the wallet is jeopardized and it would be simpler for somebody to take the coins. Better to have them all in or out.

People who use paper wallets are generally security mindful, and there are some methods for the dubious on the planet to hack your computer system. Bitcoinpaperwallet.com gives a ton of great guidance about how to print your wallets safely.

Some people have also inquired about purchasing bitcoins on eBay. Yes, it is possible, but they will be far overpriced. So, selling on eBay may appear to be a much better choice given the severe markup over market price you may see. However, just like anything that is too great to be real, this is too great to be real. As I will clarify in the next area, selling bitcoin that way is just way too dangerous.

Chapter 28: What You Should Learn about Dogecoin

Dogecoin is a cryptocurrency that was created by Billy Markus, a Portland developer.

Using the currency started as a meme-based joke where Jackson Palmer, a member of adobe systems was asked by a student to make the dogecoin idea a truth. Palmer went on and bought the dogecoin domain and created a really appealing site.

A month and half later after the currency was released to the world, it become the 3rd most important altcoin with a market cap of $53 million.

Although, it might appear complex to comprehend how the currency works, there are lots of resources that you can use to your benefit.

Research has revealed that there are many individuals who are checking out the sites using the coins. The reason there are so many people checking out the sites using the currency is since the people want to comprehend how the currency works from direct experience.

Many individuals using the currency are players and university student. These people play the games using the currency or send out cash to their good friends. The most interesting aspect of getting dogecoins is that it's extremely gratifying.

This is as when you get the currency you look like if you have gotten a ton of cash. For instance, when you are given 500 dogecoins you will view as if you have gotten a ton of cash which will give you a high self-confidence. These benefits have made dogecoin to be extremely popular and its usage has considerably increased.

The currency has also played a major social part where it has been used in raising cash for worthwhile causes. For instance, the currency helped in raising over $3,000 that was used in moneying the Jamaican bobsled group to the Sochi winter season Olympics.

After doing this, the currency played a substantial role in raising $25,000 that was used in assisting kids dealing with impairments. There are lots of other efforts that are in spot that focus on making an important difference in the society.

Although, the currency has succeeded, it has suffered certain obstacles. One problem is where the reserve bank of India warned Dogecoin users from using the currency because of the threats that ware included with it. Due to the care given by the bank, lots of people stopped using the currency.

Another obstacle is the 2013 theft where countless coins were taken throughout a hacking effort. This made some people to be over careful when using the currency.

When the majority of people come up with cryptocurrency they may too be thinking about puzzling currency. Really couple of people appear to know what it is and for some reason everybody appears to be speaking about it just as if they do. This book will ideally debunk all the elements of cryptocurrency so that by the time you're completed reading you will have a respectable idea of what it is and what it's really all about and how to purchase it

You might find that cryptocurrency is for you or you might not but at least you'll have the ability to consult with a degree of certainty and knowledge that other ones will not have.

There are many individuals who have already reached millionaire status by handling cryptocurrency. Plainly there's a ton of cash in this brand name brand-new market.

Cryptocurrency is electronic currency, brief and basic. Nevertheless, what's not so brief and basic is precisely how it comes to have value.

Unlike fiat cash, another part of what makes crypto currency important is that, like a product like silver and gold, there's only a limited amount of it. Just 21,000,000 of these incredibly intricate algorithms were produced. No more, no less. It can't be changed by printing more of it, like a federal government printing more cash to pump up the system without support. Or by a bank modifying a digital journal, something the Federal Reserve will advise banks to do to change for inflation.

Cryptocurrency is a way to acquire, sell, and invest that entirely keeps away from both federal government oversight and banking systems tracking the movement of your cash. In a world economy that is destabilized, this system can become a steady force.

Cryptocurrency also gives you a good deal of privacy. Sadly, this can result in abuse by a criminal component using crypto currency to their own ends just as routine cash can be misused. Nevertheless, it can also keep the federal government from tracking your every purchase and attacking your individual privacy.

Cryptocurrency comes in numerous kinds. Bitcoin was the very first and is the requirement from which all other cryptocurrencies pattern themselves. All are produced by careful alpha-numerical calculations from a complex coding tool. Some other cryptocurrencies are Litecoin, Namecoin, Peercoin, Dogecoin, and Worldcoin, among other ones. These are called altcoins as a generalized name. The rates of each are managed by the supply of the particular cryptocurrency and the need that the marketplace has for that currency.

The way cryptocurrency is brought into presence is rather remarkable. Unlike gold, which needs to be mined from the ground, cryptocurrency is simply an entry in a virtual journal which is saved in numerous computer systems all over the world. These entries need to be 'mined' using mathematical algorithms. Individual users or, most likely, a group of users run computational analysis to find specific series of information, called blocks. The 'miners' find information that produces a precise pattern to the cryptographic algorithm. At that point, it's applied to the series, and they have found a block. After a comparable information series on the block compares with the algorithm, the block of information has been unencrypted. The miner gets a benefit of a particular amount of cryptocurrency. As time goes on, the amount of the benefit reduces as the cryptocurrency ends up being scarcer. Contributing to that, the intricacy of the algorithms in the look for brand-new blocks is also increased. Computationally, it ends up being tougher to find a coordinating series. Both of these situations come together to reduce the speed in which cryptocurrency is created. This mimics the trouble and deficiency of mining a product like gold.

Now, anybody can be a miner. The begetters of Bitcoin made the mining tool open source, so it's totally free to anybody. Nevertheless, the computer systems they use run 24 hr a day, 7 days a week. The algorithms are incredibly intricate and the CPU is running full tilt. Lots of users have specialized computer systems made particularly for mining cryptocurrency. Both the user and the specialized computer system are called miners.

Miners (the human ones) also keep journals of deals and serve as auditors, so that a coin isn't replicated in any way. This keeps the system from being hacked and from running amok. They're paid for this work by getting brand-new cryptocurrency each week that they keep their operation. They keep their cryptocurrency in specialized files on their computer systems or other individual gadgets. These files are called wallets.

Cryptocurrency: electronic currency; also called digital currency.

Fiat cash: any legal tender; federal government backed, used in banking system.

Bitcoin: the initial and gold requirement of crypto currency.

Altcoin: other cryptocurrencies that are patterned from the exact same procedures as Bitcoin, but with small variations in their coding.

Miners: a private or group of people who use their own resources (computer systems, electrical energy, space) to mine digital coins.

Wallet: a little file on your computer system where you save your digital cash.

Conceiving the cryptocurrency system in a nutshell:

Electronic cash.

Mined by people who use their own resources to find the coins.

A steady, limited system of currency. For instance, there are only 21,000,000 Bitcoins produced for perpetuity.

Does not need any federal government or bank to make it work.

Rates is determined by the amount of the coins found and used which is integrated with the need from the general public to have them.

There are some types of crypto currency, with Bitcoin being very first and primary.

Can bring great wealth, but, like any financial investment, has dangers.

Many people find the principle of cryptocurrency to be remarkable. It's a brand-new field that could be the next cash cow for lots of them. If you find that cryptocurrency is something you wish to discover more about then you have found the right report. Nevertheless, I have hardly touched the surface area in this report. There is much, a lot more to cryptocurrency than what I have gone through here.

This digital rush of cash that is sweeping the international financiers is not only getting simpler, but also riskier by the day. While it was at first an easy peer-to-peer system for little deals, it is now used for significant financial investments and foreign high-end purchases, which has introduced more recent methods and a figured out. How does it actually work?

Bitcoin is a currency just like any other. It cannot only be used to purchase and sell, but can be used for investing and sharing, and can even be taken. While the preliminary intro of the innovation came with a desktop program, it can now be straight run through a mobile phone application, which enables you to instantly purchase, sell, trade or perhaps cash your bitcoins for dollars.

Financial investment with bitcoins has ended up being popular, with significant amounts of cash being put in every day. As a brand-new financier, the guidelines stay the exact same as investing with real money. Do not invest more than you can afford to lose, and do not invest without an objective. For each trade, keep certain turning points in mind. The 'purchase low and sell high' technique is not as simple executed as said. A great way to prosper faster when you choose to trade bitcoins, though, is to discover the technicalities. Like money financial investments, there are now some bitcoin charting tools to make a record of the marketing patterns and make forecasts to help you make financial investment choices. Even as a novice, learning how to use charting tools and how to check out charts can go a long way. A regular chart will normally consist of the opening cost, the closing cost, the greatest cost, the most affordable cost and the trading variety, which are the fundamentals you really need right before making any sale or purchase. Other parts will give you different info about the marketplace. For instance, the 'order book' includes lists of rates and amounts that bitcoin sellers want to purchase and sell.

Furthermore, brand-new financiers will usually rapidly open unprofitable positions. With this, though, remember that you need to pay a rates of interest for every single 24 hr that the position is kept open, with the exception of the very first 24 hr that are completely free. For that reason, unless you have adequate balance to cover the high rates of interest, do not keep any unprofitable position open for more than 24 hr.

While bitcoin trading still has its downsides, like deals taking too long to finish and no reversing alternative, it can benefit you considerably with investing, supplied that you take little steps in the right direction.

TOP 10 POINTERS FOR SUCCESS WITH LITECOIN

1) No Tax

When you make purchases through dollars, euros or any other federal government flat currency, you need to pay an addition amount of cash to the federal government as tax. Every buyable product has its own designated tax rate. Nevertheless, when you're buying through litecoin, sales taxes are not contributed to your purchase. This is considered as a legal form of tax evasion and is just one of the significant benefits of being a Bitcoin user.

With absolutely no tax rates, litecoin can come in convenient specifically when buying high-end products that are special to a foreign land. Such products, generally, are greatly taxed by the federal government.

2) Versatile Online Payments

litecoin is an online payment system and just like any other such system, the users of litecoin have the high-end of paying for their coins from any corner of the world that has a web connection. This means that you could be lying on your bed and buying coins rather than taking the strong pain of taking a trip to a particular bank or shop to get your work done.

Furthermore, an online payment by means of litecoin doesn't need you to fill out specifics about your individual info. For this reason, litecoin processing deals is a lot easier than those performed through U.S. Checking account and charge card.

3) Very Little Deal Charges

Costs and exchange expenses belong and parcel of basic wire transfers and worldwide purchases. litecoin is not kept track of or moderated by any intermediary organization or federal government firm. For that reason, the expenses of negotiating are kept really low as opposed to worldwide deals made by means of standard currencies

In addition to this, deals in litcoin are not understood to be time consuming since it doesn't include the problems of common permission requirements and waiting durations.

4) Hid User Identity

All litcoin deals are discrete, or to put it simply Bitcoin gives you the alternative of User privacy. litcoins resemble cash only purchases in the sense that your deals can never ever be tracked back to you and these purchases are never ever gotten in touch with your individuality. As a matter of simple fact, the litcoin address that is created for user purchases is never ever the exact same for 2 different deals.

If you want to, you do have the alternative of willingly exposing and releasing your litcoin deals but most of the times users keep their identities secret.

5) No outdoors interferences

Among the best benefits of litecoin is that it removes 3rd party disruptions. This means that federal governments, banks and other monetary intermediaries have no authority whatsoever to interfere with user deals or freeze a litecoin account. As discussed previously, litecoin is based strictly on a peer to peer system. For this reason, the users of litecoin take pleasure in greater liberty when making purchases with Bitcoins than they do when using traditional nationwide currencies.

Purchasing gold bullion with litecoin is simpler than you believe. I managed to find a really particular way to use my litecoin to purchase gold bullion each and every single month on automation. The best part is that the bitcoin I used to purchase the gold, did not even cost me anything. In simple fact, the gold I purchased was technically completely free.

I am not making presumptions or attempting to persuade anybody to run and spend all their incomes on empty guarantees. The technique I use to build up gold bullion is a truth and I use this technique each and every single day, which I will be showing you on this short article.

The following steps are included to make this a success

Start mining bitcoin

Connect your online wallet with a visa card

Save up bitcoin and purchase gold bullion

Start networking and refer people to your technique

Make affiliate commissions

6) Connect your online wallet with a visa card

Once you have found a credible business, begin mining bitcoin and send it to your online wallet to keep as much bitcoin as you perhaps can within a brief duration. Search for a bitcoin wallet business that offers their customers a visa card that can be connected to their wallet.

7) Save up litecoin and purchase gold bullion

This card can then be used to make purchases online, drawing money at a bank or making basic payments like purchasing groceries. All the deals are simply bitcoin that you are investing and none of it is originating from your real savings account. Once you have the visa card you would be in a position to acquire gold bullion online.

The next step is to find a business that sells gold bullion online and you would have the ability to pay for it using your charge card. Use the visa card I discussed previously on this post and purchase some gold bullion. Very first test the system and make sure that the gold you purchase are 24 karat gold. I would advise you purchase your gold bullion in 5 gram pieces as they are much easier to deal with when needed.

8) Start networking and refer people to your approach

There are many methods to make a very good earnings and among them is using the power of networking. Once you have managed to hold your piece of gold bullion in your hand by acquiring it with bitcoin, people would like to know how you did it. Clarify to them your method and they will follow.

9) Make affiliate commissions

If you have picked businesses within the bitcoin and gold bullion market that offers their customers an affiliate commission, you would be making a great passive earnings from your networking efforts. This is just some of my approaches I use to build an online organisation that I know would last for several years to come

10) Earn money online and transform them to Bitcoin

Actually believe it or not, it is still a lot easier to make United States Dollars! You can then exchange these dollars you produce Bitcoin at any of the exchanges just like Bitstamp or Coinbase if you lie in the United States.

Make Bitcoin Straight in the Bitcoin economy

There is a little but really lively community where you can do most jobs, but at a much littler scale. For example, you can use up a part-time job for Bitcoin on Coinality or you can wind up with a little gig on Coingig. These are reality equivalent of sites like Elance and Fiverr but in the Bitcoin environment.

Marketing

The marketing market in the Bitcoin economy is, not remarkably, quite robust. This is since there are lots of brand-new Bitcoin based services that keep turning up all the time and they all really need a really good marketing network.

CoinURL enables you to position Google AdSense styled advertisements on your site and other services like Bitads lets marketers quote for banner space on your blog site. There is also a-ads that enables you to earn money through advertisement impressions without reference to the clicks (so it isn't Pay Per Click). If you're a publisher - blog writer or web designer, you can make some Bitcoins through this path.

Going Social

There are sites that will pay you for your activity. CoinChat is maybe the best recognized site in this classification. It pays users several milli-Bitcoins for talking on their site. These are random and managed by an algorithm that takes into consideration your activity and how well you're adding to the conversations at hand.

Another method which a ton of Bitcoin lovers make some Bitcoin is by selling their forum signatures at Bitcointalk forums. There are a really good number of marketers who want to do this, and for the socially active member who values interaction through this forum (it is the exact same forum through which Satoshi Nakamoto introduced Bitcoin to the world), selling signatures can be profitable.

Made in the USA
Monee, IL
15 December 2021

85765959R00063